THE ENTERTAINERS

An Omnibus of

Edited by Mark C. Hewitt

LLL PUBLICATIONS

Limited First Edition of 1000 books.
Published 1998 by LLL Publications.
Lewes Live Literature, All Saints Centre,
Friars Walk, Lewes, East Sussex BN7 2LE.
Tel. 01273 476686 Fax 01273 477583.
E-mail: flo@pavilion.co.uk

Edited by Mark C. Hewitt.
Book Design by Greg Daville.

Printed by The Bridge Press
Bridge House, Robinson Road, Newhaven, East Sussex BN9 9BL.

© Individual copyright remains with authors, publishers or artists as per acknowledgement.
© This collection, Lewes Live Literature Publications.

ISBN 0 9532507 0 9

The right of Mark C. Hewitt to be identified as the editor of this work has been asserted by him in accordance with the Copyright, Designs & Patents Act 1988.

All rights reserved. No part of this book may be reproduced, stored in a retrieval system, or transmitted in any form, or by any means, electronic, mechanical, photocopying or otherwise without prior written permission from LLL Publications.

Lewes Live Literature gratefully acknowledges support for the publication of this book from the Asham Literary Endowment Trust and the National Lottery through the Arts Council of England.

Introduction

Lewes Live Literature is a promoter of literary, poetic, artistic and musical events and exhibitions based in the historic capital of East Sussex. All of the contributors to this wide-ranging omnibus have been involved, in one way or another, with these activities. Many, but by no means all, live within this area of Sussex. Others have become involved in projects specifically by invitation.

The work in this book is not the result of any particular editorial stance. The diversity of approaches, styles and sensibilities is simply a reflection of the range of events that Lewes Live Literature has promoted since it was founded in 1995. Not just writers and poets but artists, composers, musicians, cartoonists and comedians. Many of the contributors are skilled, recognised practitioners in more than one of these disciplines. The images featured in this anthology mostly relate to a series of exhibitions, *Marriages of Word & Image*, that have explored aspects of the relationship between literature and the visual arts.

My thanks firstly to all those herein represented who have so generously contributed their work to this collection. Secondly to those others who have helped behind the scenes at events over the years. My thanks also to the funding bodies that have supported Lewes Live Literature financially since its inception, in particular South East Arts Board, Lewes Town and District Councils, the Asham Literary Endowment Trust, the Arts Council of England and the many local business sponsors that have supported events during the Lewes Festival, in particular Cliffe Bookshop. And last but not least, my thanks to all those of you that have bought copies of this book. All profits will go towards the promotion of bigger and better events and the development of new projects.

Mark Hewitt
Editor
Artistic Director, Lewes Live Literature

Acknowledgments

Peter Abbs: In Defence of the Raven, Fallen Man with One Wing & Wittgenstein's Furniture also published (with accompanying prints by **Lynne Gibson**) as a limited signed edition of fine hand-printed booklets by Geoffrey Treneman's Snake River Press. The poems (without the prints) can also be found in *Personae and other selected poems* (Skoob Books, 1995). **John Agard**: The Devil's Advice to Old Couplers & Have a Chickpea on me, Mahatma Ghandi were first published in *From the Devil's Pulpit* (Bloodaxe, 1997), Love Calls Us Back from Simplification was first published in *A Stone's Throw from Embankment* (Royal Festival Hall, 1993). **Julian Bell**: poem previously unpublished. Self Portrait courtesy Francis Kyle Gallery. **Peter Blegvad**: Amateur interview first published in the pamphlet *Amateur* (Amateur Enterprises, New York 1977); On Numinous Objects and their Manufacture & Morphological Tables first published in *Re Records Quarterly* Volume 2 No.2, September 1985. **Gordon Bowker**: article previously unpublished. Photograph of Lowry courtesy of the Lowry Archive, University of British Columbia. **Martin Cooper**: Torridonian Sandstone from *Fire On The Mountain* (Cliffe Bookshop, 1997). **Peter Copley**: article previously unpublished. **Lol Coxhill**: scrap previously unpublished. **Greg Daville**: extract from novel in progress. **John Dowie**: The Astrologer And The Ant first published in the pamphlet *Bits* (U Productions, 1995). **Andy Gammon**: images previously unpublished. **Doj Graham**: article previously unpublished. **Tony Haase**: monologue previously unpublished. **David Harsent**: poems from The Hoop of the World, (originally part of the libretto for an opera), previously unpublished. **Jonathan Harvey**: manuscript page from Three Sketches for solo cello, published in its completed form by Faber Music. **Drew Hewitt**: lecture previously unpublished. **Mark C. Hewitt**: works previously unpublished. **Pierre Hollins**: from the series of *Guru* cartoons previously published in The Fortean Times. **Nicki Jackowska**: The Woman Who Mistook Her Father for an Irishman and Marilyn on the Mountain from *Lighting a Slow Fuse - New and Selected Poems* (Enitharmon, 1998). The Woman Who Mistook Her Father for an Irishman was also previously published in *Poetry Review*. **Di Kaufman**: images previously unpublished. **Mimi Khalvati**: poems from *Entries on Light* (Carcanet Press Ltd. 1997). **Peter Messer**: Boatbuilding and Astronomy previously reproduced in Artist's Review, November 1997. **Grace Nichols**: Long Man and First Generation Monologue first published in *Sunris*, (Virago, 1996), reproduced with permission of Curtis Brown Ltd, London, on behalf of Grace Nichols. **Stephen Plaice**: story previously unpublished. **Paul Taylor**: photograph previously unpublished. **David Thomas**: text previously unpublished. (©1997 Hearpen Music.) **Carolyn Trant**: text and images previously published in artist's book *Gawain* (Parvenu Press, 1997).

Tom Walker: images previously unpublished. **Mutahar Williams**: Mountain Train previously published in *Staple* magazine. Other poems previously unpublished.

Biographical Portrait Credits

Peter Abbs by **Mark Lovell**, John Agard by **Paul Taylor**, Julian Bell by **Julian Bell**, Peter Blegvad by **Cassey King**, Gordon Bowker by **Martin Durrant**, Peter Copley by **Richard Lemon**, Andy Gammon by **Andy Gammon**, Lynne Gibson by **Keith Wilson**, David Harsent by **Simon Harsent**, Jonathan Harvey by **Maurice Foxall**, Drew Hewitt by **Drew Hewitt**, Mark Hewitt by **Andy Gammon**, Pierre Hollins by **Rollo**, Di Kaufman by **Di Kaufman**, Mimi Khalvati by **Keith Blandin**, Grace Nichols by **Gillian Cargill,** Tom Walker by **Tom Walker**.

Engravings of dancing figures by Johann Georg Puschner from New and Curious School of Theatrical Dancing by Gregorio Lambranzi, (Nuremburg 1716).

Preface

The View from the Hill

Lewes - the old hill - has always attracted to it the wayward and the bolshie, the political and religious dissenters. It is currently stuffed with artists. It may have been an Iron Age burial site. It was certainly visited by Marilyn Monroe. I've heard rumours of a photo of Picasso on Lewes station.

Once a year the Bonfire Boys set the streets alight. The rest of the year, a great many spend at least part of the day weaving from pub to pub, each an island of eccentricity, full of chat. And if anything goes a bit bendy, or if you turn a corner in a dark twitten only to bump into the coalman dressed as Vlad the Impaler, you shrug and say "It's just Lewes".

The town, once you acclimatise to its skank rhythms, is propelled along by the kind of lunatic visions, revelatory insights, genuinely funny musings, archaeological detective work, free-form discourse and playful wordsmithery on display in this nugget-studded volume.

Not all the artistes involved in its production actually reside in the town's precinct, but something of the place's curious mixture of eccentric menace and flawless laughter has rubbed off on this collection.

Welcome to The Entertainers.

John May
17th February 1998

Contents

Peter Abbs	In Defence of the Raven	11
	Fallen Man with One Wing	12
	Wittgenstein's Furniture	13
John Agard	The Devil's Advice to Old Couplers	14
	Have a Chickpea on Me, Mahatma Ghandi	15
	"Love Calls Us Back from Simplification"	16
Julian Bell	From a Clearance	17
Peter Blegvad	On Numinous Objects and Their Manufacture	18
	An Interview (Amateur Science Fiction)	22
Gordon Bowker	The Last Days of Malcolm Lowry	28
Martin Cooper	Torridonian Sandstone	32
Peter Copley	What Sort of Music Do You Write?	33
Lol Coxhill	Scrap	36
Greg Daville	Harbinger's Net (A Work in Progress)	37
John Dowie	The Astrologer And The Ant	52
Doj Graham	Nine Men's Morris	54
Tony Haase	The Black Room	59
David Harsent	The Seabirds' Chorus	75
	The Scientists' Song	76
Drew Hewitt	Berts, Toms, Jacks and a Sig	78

Mark C. Hewitt	Old Man River	98
	Purgations III	99
	Purgations X	100
	Purgations XII	101
Pierre Hollins	Guru	102
Nicki Jackowska	The Woman Who Mistook Her Father For An Irishman	103
	Marilyn on the Mountain	104
Mimi Khalvati	Entries on Light	106
Grace Nichols	First Generation Monologue	109
	Long Man	112
Stephen Plaice	The Holy Spirit	114
David Thomas	Untitled	129
Mutahar Williams	Socks	132
	The Old King	133
	Mountain Train	134

Biographical Details   136

List of Illustrations

Section One	*Black and White Plates 1-8*

Jonathan Harvey Manuscript Page
Andy Gammon Illuminated Man No.1
 Illuminated Man No.5
Peter Blegvad First Morphological Table
 Second Morphological Table
 Third Morphological Table
 Key to Morphological Tables
Paul Taylor George and Nelson

Section Two	*Colour Plates 9-16*

Greg Daville House of the Spirits
Lynne Gibson The Quester
 The Starwort Shirt
 Icarus at the Big Top
Drew Hewitt Cirkus Family
 This Sporting Life
 The Levitator
Greg Daville Proposed Monument to Love

Section Three	*Colour Plates 17-24*

Di Kaufman Sitter
Peter Messer Boatbuilding and Astronomy
 River of Secret Fish
Carolyn Trant Autumn
 I Am Not The Hero
Tom Walker All Who Come Here Come Here Alone
 Ridiculous Ramshackle Edifice
 Submerged Cathedral

In Defence of the Raven

And it came to pass at the end of forty days that Noah opened the window of the ark which he had made: and he sent forth a raven, which went forth to and fro, until the waters were dried up from off the earth. Also he sent forth a dove.

Genesis Ch. 8 v.6-8.

It did not leave at once. For two hours
Or more it perched on the ark,
Eyeing the waves and the slanting horizon:
A dark witness under storm clouds.

Nor, when it finally left, did it go lightly.
At first, unsure of direction, it flew
Without grace. An equivocation of wings,
A mere inch above drowning water.

By all means cherish the dove. It returned
Loyally with good news in its beak.
So make it your icon on banners of peace
And hang them over the warring cities.

But, at night, as you try to sleep, remember
Far horizons, black holes, exploded nova stars;
Remember the curved edge of God's
Incommensurable mind - where the raven flies.

Peter Abbs

Fallen Man with One Wing

Only the youngest brother, whose sleeve she had had no time to finish,
had a swan's wing instead of an arm...
From the Grimms' *The Six Swans*

Please don't ask who I am. I'm a stranger here.
Have no parents. No clear past. No fixed address.
I am a catalogue of questions with only riddles
For answers. I limp boundaries, stumble through war-zones
Where history meanders, breaks off, locks on itself.
I struggle each day to keep two feet on the ground.
Death sticks in the palm of my hand like a hand-grenade.

From where did I fall? From what height to what depth?
What time was it then? Was it night? Were there stars
In the vault of the sky? Or was it the heart of day?
Were there strips of blue out over the sea?
Was anyone there? Did they record my fall?
All the bureaucratic forms, all the files are blank.
Then, who spun the garment which half covers my skin?
Who draped it over my head? It nettles and stings.

Amnesiac under the sun, the more I question
The less I understand. And what is this wing where
An arm should be? This shaming thing. This dark
Impediment. And who put a star on my brutish brow
To mark me out for what inscrutable purpose?
It burns. I touch it. There's gold on my hand.
I'm on trial here. Much of the time I'm out
Of my mind. I scrawl notes when I can.

It is evening. The sun falls through amber.
We could be near the end of Winter.

Peter Abbs

Wittgenstein's Furniture

Wittgenstein's furniture is all over the place.
His severe steel chair lies on its back;
The clean windows are blasted to smithereens.
The hands of time have been torn off. The clock
Ticks absurdly. It has a vacant face.

A formal note on the stripped floor reads:
The limits of my language are the limits

Of my world. Sheathed in sequins, the boy
Glides through the dazzling light, his hair
Silver and gold from speechless dreams.
Fifty feet up and more, his hands grip air
Before he returns to dive through his shadow

Effortlessly. Mesmerised, the spectators scream.
Bowing, unburnt Icarus leaves the ring.

The Devil's Advice to Old Couplers

So what if his prick
can no longer raise its senile
head. Whisper something vile
into his octogenarian ear
to tinkle the glass of his spine.

So what if her bosom
has now lowered its flag.
Her mind still basks in talk of shag.
And you can at least salute
her with your shrivelled root.

Come all ye couplers.
Now the curtain is drawn
set fire to your autumnal straws.
Frolic among a haystack of wrinkles.
Seize time by the crotch.
Make the Grim Reaper blush.

Or must I repeat in those doting ears of thine
that Sara at ninety saw pregnancy signs
and Abraham at ninety-nine was circumcised?

Have a Chickpea on Me, Mahatma Gandhi

Mahatma Gandhi, venerable Babu,
I'd like a word with you.

You who taught the English the virtue
of cotton; the politics of salt;
and the omnipotence of chickpea.

What's all this I hear about you lying half-
dhoti-clad among honey-skinned virgins
to rigidly test your celibacy?

Between you, me and the Raj,
I'm sure you must have been randy
but 0 so beautiful at camouflage.

"Love Call Us Back from Simplification"

(For Eavan Boland, who made this inspiring comment during her poetry reading/talk as part of an Irish Womens' Day at the Voice Box, Royal Festival Hall, April '92)

Out of the mouth of an Irish woman
pebbles of love play ducks and drakes
across the April face of the river Thames.

Tonight the voice will not be boxed-in
by man-made dimensions or canons of sin.
The tongue revelling in connection.

Let griot seaniche tinker obeahwoman
raise a glass to the health of contradiction.
Now Carrickfergus merge with Caribbean.

Love calls us back from simplification.

To reduce a nation to a label
To reduce a race to an assumption
To reduce a face to a formula of black and white

To hang a stereotype around the heart
To build a wall with stones of conviction
To let the map dictate affection

To allow boundaries their frozen dance
To grant frontiers their fixity of expression
To make a monument of an ism.

But love calls us back from simplification.
Tonight in a room above a river above a city
a poet is sharing the bread of her words

and we walking out blessed with resonance.

John Agard

From a Clearance

The doors fly wide, flooding the house with chill.
The clouds yield to blue, whipped from the east.
The way lies ahead, unmetalled and ill-frequented.
The birds take to their kingdom, their raucous swirl released

To jolt the dilatory, those who said, we are exempt,
Marginal, peripheral, slantwise to history;
Lichen on the roofridge blazons out our rights,
A disregarded zodiac pivots on our appletree;

Those who roughride stolen cars beyond the manor wall
Those also who proceeded with due caution;
Those with bowed heads, dreaming at their spades
Those who kept vigil for the wrong revolution;

All are filling hipflasks, grabbing valuables
For new accommodations with the wind
That comes as corrective, that stays as corrosive
Driving us, pinched and raw-skinned,

Some to the pickings of rootless urban infill,
Some to the pickings of roads. The queue
Around the charabancs, the siren khaki charabancs,
Turns ugly. Shift! Chance won't wait! But you,

Hesitant in your doorway, hobbled child,
Brimming as a tear for charity to catch,
If there were a relic, if there were a charm
Against the powers that planned this, I would latch

Upon your hovering breath, quickening, slowing;
Your pupils, flecked by black wings swooping;
Your full and hollow ribcage, wholly attending;
Your grip on the handle, free arm drooping.

*The eagerness of objects to
be what we are afraid to do*

*Cannot help but move us Is
this willingness to be a motive*

*in us what we reject?"
(from Interior, Frank O'hara)*

On Numinous Objects and Their Manufacture
(Part One of a Potentially Endless Work)

Objects proliferate as never before, but they are mostly dead husks, the shells of things, wherein no daemon resides [1]. We own them merely, or covet them, we are not nourished. Meanwhile, the fundamental appetite for *numinous objects* [2] grows ravenous. Nevermind that it remains unconscious in most citizens and unacknowledged by the authorities. Only numinous objects can make possible the communication between people and so-called "dead matter" [3], which must be established if we wish to avert calamity.

I am not here referring to *fetishes*, which are a means to evoke a system of belief and not properly ends in themselves. Nor am I referring to fantasy constructs like, for example, the ship made of nail-parings described in Norse mythology. This ship is, undeniably, a fine-thing, but it is only feebly numinous compared to a block of sodium in a meadow, its edges mollified by the tongues of cows into a lopsided loaf like snow. And, while my more sceptical readers may scoff, it is a fact that if this salt-lick be removed from the meadow and placed in a confined enclosure or, better still, sealed into a lead container, its numinous charge will be boosted many fold [4].

---

1. Daemon - *the animating spirit of a place or thing. Cf. the painter, Giorgio de Chirico's dictate: "One must discover the daemon in everything."*
2. Numinous - *invested with power or spirit.*
3. Guy Davenport: *"... science and poetry from the Renaissance forward have been trying to discover what is alive and what isn't. In science the discovery spanned three centuries, from Gassendi to Niels Bohr, and the answer is that everything is alive." Davenport also quotes Einstein: "... every clod of earth, every feather, every speck of dust is a prodigious reservoir of entrapped energy." (from Olson, in* The Geography of the Imagination*)*
4. Cf. Leonora Carrington: *"The explosion... had momentarily dispersed the powers that always gathered around the Cup in enclosed areas. This is a magic law and true for nearly all charged objects." (from* The Hearing Trumpet*)*

It may be, as some have theorized, that the object, "au naturel" or in its "accumulator"[5], is numinous to the degree that it functions as a "mirror of the spirit", to the degree that you or I can imaginatively see something of ourselves, something we do not ordinarily have a name for or an image of, made objective in it. That *salt* can function as a mirror of *anything,* especially when sealed in lead, will smack of blatant hocus-pocus to the sceptics - but it is in such unlikely ways that the imagination actually works.

A numinous object is charged like a condenser. It distorts induction and resonates ambiguously. In Surrealist parlance, it is "convulsive", with the power to abrogate definition from its surroundings and become the solitary and radiant focus, the omphalos or navel, of an entire world. An object with sufficient numinous charge can stop time.

The numinous objects which already exist in our environment are easily overlooked by our harrassed and addled species. Education is the remedy, teaching people of all ages to resist distraction and become sensitive to the subtle radiation emanating from these items (which often masquerade as common refuse on the street). I imagine students returning, bright-eyed and exultant, from expeditions to dumps, factories, zoos, firing-ranges, hospitals, quarries, ships, farms, forests, cinemas, circuses, cemeteries and recording studios with their eclectic spoil. Objects thus collected would be tested, graded and catalogued before being made available to the public from a chain of lending libraries.

Besides numinous "found objects", fresh numinous objects must be manufactured. To meet this need a new science is being evolved here at the offices of Amateur. The plates which follow illustrate the first phase of this work: discovering the morphologies or forms most conducive to numinosity, I am still compiling the list of materials of which these forms or objects might be compounded. The selection is *vast,* and the distinction is critical, in terms of numinosity, between a ball, let us say, of *snow*, and one the same size, made of, for example, *soluble glass*[6] - although both balls, viewed from a certain distance, might otherwise be twins.

---

5. *Cf. Wilhelm Reich and his "accumulators" and "boosters" (of "orgone energy").*
6. *One reason the list of materials is potentially endless is that science keeps inventing new, potentially numinous, matter. Dr. Cyril Drake, for example, "accidentally made a glass that dissolved in water." "Without silicon, using phosphorous, calcium and sodium oxides", the ingredients in Dr. Drake's soluble glass can be adjusted to make it dissolve as swiftly or as slowly as required, "from a few minutes up to ten years."*

Peter Blegvad

How would an alchemist seeking the *lapis* or Philosopher's Stone picture it in his mind? (The Tractatus aureus says the precious Stone is "altogether vile", but aside from that…) Would he imagine an amorphous lump, a perfect sphere, or a brick? Would it be oily or dry, dull or polished, cold or warm to the touch? Would it be fused into a dense solid or porous, ventilated like a honeycomb? Such grossly materialistic speculations demean the spiritual associations the Stone evokes, no doubt, but in seeking the recipe for numinous objects I have found it useful to ask myself such questions…

To return to the morphologies - I have deliberately restricted the choice to *basic* forms and objects, at least for my first tentative experiments. If an object can be inserted into the phrase "the object is _____-shaped", (e.g. *cigar*, *bullet*, *barrel* or *teardrop*-shaped) it will usually qualify for selection. Other objects qualify as nearly archetypal "signs for themselves" (e.g. gallows or gibbett ү, coffin ⟨⟩, and house ⌂ [7]) It is a basic "building block" quality that I seek. Certain forms, by their inclusion, automatically disqualify others. *Hourglass*, for instance, renders *Dumbell* superfluous, because the latter ∞ is too nearly the former on its side.

I have separated the forms and objects into three categories: those composed entirely of straight lines ("Straight"); those in whose lineaments curves and circles are involved ("Curved"); and, lastly, those indefinite units of matter, the humble blob, chunk, chip, lump, heap, hill, etc. which, while sometimes suggesting the quantity of matter involved, do not imply more than a very approximate form ("Amorphous"). The reader will notice that some two-dimensional figures have been included on the Tables, and even a few negative shapes (holes, cracks, and crenellations). They are there because it seems certain that an aperture or apertures could contribute to the numinosity of an object, and that a two-dimensional tattoo or other type of marking might do likewise.

Many forms and objects are missing that should be included. Some of the forms currently under consideration are pictured on the last page of this article. Should more letter-shapes qualify? L,T,V,O,S,U,X and Z now seem to me to be all *basic* forms, maybe the rest are too. Sometimes I wonder if a numinous object could not therefore be a *word*…

It may transpire that unless I find the appropriate *context* in which to place a finished object, it will not "convulse", it's numinosity will remain dormant.

7. House not pictured in the Second Morphological Table.

Morphological Tables see Plates 4 - 7.

Conventional gallery design since the middle of the century would indicate that the aesthetic qualities of an *art* object are supposedly savoured best in an antiseptic interior and under electric lamplight. But an object such as I propose to manufacture, and which I do not think of simply as "art", might require a specific site, a specific hour of day or night, specific support "props", weather conditions, and so on before "its soul, its whatness, leaps to us from the vestment of its appearance" [8] and it becomes numinous.

8. James Joyce, describing the "epiphany" of an object.

AMATEUR

AN INTERVIEW (AMATEUR SCIENCE FICTION)

Q : Is it numinousness, numinessence, or numinosity?

A : It's like luminous.

Q : You say numinosity?

A : I do.

Q : And when a thing is numinous it exudes an air of mystery, of sanctity?

A : Of _energy_. It appears charged.

Q : I see. And may I ask how you programmed the computer to recognize and measure the numinosity of these queer items, the "voltaic piles"[1] for instance?

A : Twenty of us toiled at it night and day for eleven months. Into the UNIVAC, known to us as Maud, we fed everything from arcana pertaining to Zahirs[2] to a catalogue of army-surplus equipage, from lavish colour-plates of fish lures to a tea-stained pamphlet on numismatics. 600 miles of magnetic tape we fed into her! Thank God Maud is a fast learner or we'd still be at it. One morning she was taken with a cadence we were feeding her of Gertrude Stein's: "a lightning cooky, a single wide open and exchanged box filled with the same little sac that shines." Her console went dark a moment, next thing we knew she was drawing up plans for the construction of Stein's sac and demonstrating by means of an elegant equation that once built, 69% of sac's numinosity would be attributable to the "potent triad" embodied in it, by which she meant its Familiarity, Diminution and Radiance. Despite the early hour we broke out champagne. What relief to know those eleven gruelling months hadn't been in vain!

1. These are stacks, from $6\frac{1}{2}$ in. to 12 ft. high, of discs of diverse materials (yeast, linoleum, silver, wax, wool, etc.) all with a central perforation allowing access to a "spine" either of lead or zinc which runs the length of the pile and prevents it toppling.

2. "beings or things which possess the terrible virtue of being unforgettable and whose image finally drives people mad." - J.L. Borges

Peter Blegvad

Q : I understand the fourth and fifth months were particularly trying for Maud.

A : Indeed. During that time she was fed exclusively on case histories of insane persons. It was necessary she be taught to see even the most common objects become "smooth *LOAF* as metal, so cut off, so detached from each other, so illuminated and tense that they inspired terror."[1] It was some time before Maud was her old self again. As a kind of ther- *PLANK OR SLAB* apy she was tutored in the precipitation of that sequence of recognitions which culminates in what James Joyce called the "epiphany" of an object - when "Its soul, its whatness, leaps to us from the vestment of its appearance." *PIPE* Pride in her skill at this sport did much to restore her.

WAND, ROD OR DOWEL

Q : Will you tell us what was the purpose of all this?

A : To enable Maud to design her own objects. Programming was planned to inculcate criteria by which she could select qualities most conducive to numinosity. *WEDGE* And it more or less succeeded. Every evening for the past six months she has presented her selections in a succinct recipe describing a single object which I then attempt to realize in my shop.

Q : Can you describe how an object e- *COIN* volves in Maud's mind?

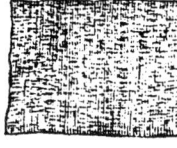

A : By a process of gradual division. Her first conception of the object may be no more than that its surface curves, that it is portable and compounded of some miner- al substance. While "curved, portable, min- *BLANKET* eral" conjures a pretty nebulous image to the average consciousness, Maud senses only its pot-

1."Autobiography of a Schizophrenic Girl" - M. Sechehaye

Peter Blegvad   23

ential which is naturally very high. The energy thus generated engages the next in a series of circuit "levels" on each of which Maud's choices get correspondingly more specific. After a tedious ascent _SPIT_ through at least 20 such levels Maud prints out a finished recipe - for example: Vll - a3. Mm. XXX B-43ff.22gr. HH*i* ++Pk. This code describes a manganese puck and specifies its circumference, thickness, weight, texture and temperature.

Diffi- _{PELLET OR PILL} culties may arise as an object approaches definition. Maud may decide that a hemisphere, say, of cellophane must not be empty. So the process begins again to determine precisely what it should contain.

Finished objects are presented to Maud for a critical "scan". 9 times out of 10 she _FAN_ can discern in them no virtú and so destroys them. Occasionally she senses numinosity latent in one and this is perceptible only to her. Twice we have had objects invested with charges so active that goggles and asbestos suits were required in order to stand in the same room _WHORL OR GYRE_ with them.

Q : Then why did you say earlier that the venture was only "more or less" successful?

A : We anticipated a whole line of numinous items and have had but two! The reason for _CRESCENT_ this is clearly that we were constrained to ignore the absolutely central factor of context. The number of variables would have been too vast even for Maud. Therefore the objects are con- _CLOUD_ ceived of as existing in a vacuum or rather in the pure negation of context. It irks us all no end. In a comedy I saw as a child Harlequin is made to remark

Peter Blegvad

that something is "as out of place as a piece of cheese in a library." Whenever Maud destroys an object, one, it may be, that I've been a week or more in the cellar manufacturing, this line comes to mind. For who's to say but that an object which seems to lack salience here in the lab might be powerfully numinous in a niche, say, among dictionaries in the Bibliotheque Nationale?

⚷ ♆ ♄ ☽ ☊ ⊕

"His breasts are full of milk and his bones are moistened with marrow" (Job 21:24)

Peter Blegvad

The Last Days of Malcolm Lowry

When Malcolm Lowry died in 1958, he died in obscurity. No obituary appeared in Britain, though the Brighton Argus carried a brief report.

> One evening last week Mrs. Marjorie Lowry, of [White] Cottage, Ripe, tried to stop her 47-year-old writer-husband, Clarence, from starting on the gin. She smashed the bottle on the floor. And he hit her. Afraid, Mrs Lowry fled next door and did not go back to the cottage until 9 o'clock the next morning. When she did she found her husband dead. This was the story told at the Eastbourne Inquest, when the Coroner, Dr A.C. Sommerville, recorded a verdict of death by misadventure. Mrs Lowry said her husband had been treated in hospital for alcoholism, but had been discharged last year as incurable.
> "When he hit me," she said, "he was under the influence and in a bad temper." PC William Ford said he found Mr. Lowry on the floor beside his bed. Near him was a smashed gin bottle and a smashed orange squash bottle. *A bottle of 20 sodium amytal sleeping tablets belonging to his wife was missing.* This was found later, empty.
> "In the house," said PC Ford, "I found a number of bottles containing tablets prescribed to Mrs Lowry."
> Medical evidence showed that Mr Lowry died from acute barbiturate poisoning associated with a state of chronic alcoholism.

The story omitted the main cause of death - 'Inhalation of stomach contents', a common death of alcoholics who mix drink and barbiturates. He had choked on his own vomit.

The *Argus*'s 'Clarence Lowry' was christened Clarence Malcolm Lowry but he preferred the name Malcolm, and he was the author of one of the century's greatest novels, *Under the Volcano*. He had moved to Ripe after 20 years abroad, mostly in North America. Like Lawrence, finding England uncongenial to the creative artist he had chosen exile. So how did he come to die in Ripe?

Lowry was born in New Brighton, Cheshire, in 1909, the youngest of four sons of a prosperous Liverpool cotton broker. He attended the Leys School, Cambridge, where he discovered writing, jazz and alcohol. At seventeen he left school to go to sea as a deckhand on a freighter trading to Yokohama, toting a ukulele and a notebook. On board he was tormented by the crew, but from this came his first novel, *Ultramarine*. In 1929 he visited America for tutoring by the poet Conrad Aiken, from whose novel *Blue Voyage* he borrowed heavily for his own book. The amoral, hard-drinking Aiken powerfully influenced the impressionable Lowry, and up at St. Catherine's College, Cambridge, later that year, he neglected his studies and played the alcoholic poet. In his first term, while drunk, he helped a friend, Paul Fitte, gas himself and was lucky to escape prosecution. Guilt over this haunted him ever afterwards, and he often drank to forget what had happened. Alcohol and remorse drove him eventually to write a great novel, but on occasions also tipped him into madness.

Ultramarine, published in 1933, received mixed reviews, and he grew disenchanted with England. He married a young American, Jan Gabrial, in Paris in 1934, and settled with her in New York. After two years struggling with a new novel, he ended up in the psychiatric ward of Bellevue Hospital, an experience which gave him *Lunar Caustic*, a surrealistic vision of the lunatic city through the eyes of a deranged alcoholic. Accused of plagiarism, he grew wary of publishing anything, and despite writing ceaselessly over the next ten years, got almost nothing into print.

In October 1936, the Lowrys left for Mexico, and Lowry was immediately spellbound by its mysterious culture and strange cult of death. He also discovered *mescal*, which caused him to hallucinate and occasionally go beserk. When Jan left him, he added the theme of deserted lover to that of self-destructive alcoholic in a new novel he had begun. Over the next eight years *Under the Volcano* grew into a great Faustian novel about the last day in the life of Geoffrey Firmin, an alcoholic ex British Consul, who has sold his soul to the demon drink and is hell-bent on self-destruction. Set on the Mexican Day of the Dead, 1938, this dazzling novel ends with one of the finest passages in literature - a great crescendo of vivid imagery where the Consul foresees the coming European holocaust. Published in 1947, the novel became a bestseller in America and was hailed as a work of genius. In England its reception was lukewarm and it was soon remaindered.

Lowry finished the book in 1945 while living in a waterside shack in British Colombia - an idyllic setting for him to indulge his passions for swimming and wildlife. Following his American success, he wrote the subtly allusive short stories in *Hear Us O Lord From Heaven Thy Dwelling Place*, and another Mexican novel, *Dark as the Grave Wherein my Friend is Laid*. He also devised an ambitious scheme, *The Voyage that Never Ends*, incorporating all his work and "attempting to give delirium a form". But he was diverted into writing a Canadian novel, *October Ferry to Gabriola*, which was rejected by his American publisher. This rejection crushed him, and in 1954, with Margerie, his second wife (an ex-Hollywood silent film actress), he moved to Europe where he collapsed mentally. Finally Margerie persuaded him to return to England where medical treatment was free.

In 1956, Lowry was treated for alcoholism at Wimbledon's Atkinson Morley Hospital. His psychiatrist, Dr. Michael Raymond, subjected him to aversion therapy, apparently curing him. Needing a quiet place to live and work, they found The White Cottage in Ripe, which Margerie thought 'miraculous' - three miles from any station but just an hour and a half by train from London. She wrote to a friend;

> It has living room. dining room (which will be Malc's workroom,) huge country kitchen, dairy, on first floor 2 bedrooms, *bath* on second floor, & attic bedroom & storeroom on 3rd floor. Front rooms look across meadow, with sheep and thatched roof farm, brook, & up to the Great South Downs. We have a walled garden with flowers, & kitchen garden where I can grow lettuce, herbs, etc...2 of the houses in our town are in the Domesday Book but you won't find the town on any map, it's too small.

They moved there on 7 February 1956. In a small village the Lowrys were a distinctly odd couple. Malcolm was short, top-heavy and red-faced, with staring blue eyes, a mop of unruly copper-coloured hair and a sailor's rolling gait. He had an odd tendency to wander the lanes talking to hedgerows. Margerie was an exotic Hollywoodish creature, always perfectly made-up and immaculately dressed. She was somewhat histrionic, believed she had married a genius, and lost patience with anyone not fascinated by her favourite topic, 'the Lowrys'. Finding her 'impossible', Malcolm's friends were reluctant to visit, so his life in Ripe was somewhat lonely.

One person who liked both Lowrys was 'Winnie' Mason, their elderly landlady, who occupied the adjoining cottage. She charged them a modest rent, and arranged for someone to cook and clean for them. In Margerie's absence, Malcolm stayed at the Rectory, which he swore was haunted by a phantom billiard ball, which bumped down the stairs in the middle of the night, step by ghostly step.

He continued work on *October Ferry*, but found abstinence increasingly difficult. Margerie had continued drinking and was drunk most evenings. When she and a friend, Lord Peter Churchill, sat knocking back the gin and saying, "How wise you are to leave this stuff alone," his resistance finally broke and he gave in to what he called his 'imp of the perverse'. Now alternately in a drunken stupor or violently raving, he was banned from his local pub in Ripe. Taken to Brighton Hospital, he was turfed out for being disruptive, and returned to the Atkinson Morley under Dr Raymond. There Margerie complained that Malcolm was helplessly dependent on her and had grown paranoid, thinking people were plotting against him or following him. She said she was very afraid of his violence. Malcolm told the doctor it was Margerie who was drinking to excess and flying into hysterical rages, sometimes tearing up his manuscripts.

Although he enjoyed jousting verbally with his psychiatrists (one exclaimed, "Let me get away from your Satanic tongue!"), after more therapy, he made good progress. On one visit, however, Margerie threatened to have him committed and return to California. But encouraged by Dr Raymond, Malcolm was soon able to dress himself and occasionally go out of the hospital unaccompanied. When he was discharged home to Ripe, the doctor felt he was finally cured and no longer so reliant on Margerie. He was even able to take the bus alone to Lewes, spend a day there, and never once be tempted into one of its welcoming pubs.

In June 1957, the Lowrys took a holiday in the Lake District. When they returned home, Malcolm seemed strangely disturbed. On the night of 26th June, they walked to the Yew Tree pub at Chalvington, where they spent a quarrelsome evening, Margerie becoming hysterically angry when he bought a bottle of gin. The landlord remembered her leaving in tears, Lowry tottering after her, clutching his bottle.

According to Margerie, as they sat listening to a BBC radio concert in their bedroom that evening, Malcolm consumed half the gin, and when she protested he grew angry. When she smashed the bottle, he attacked her, so she fled next door to Mrs Mason's, and spent the night there. Next morning, she returned to find him dead on the bedroom floor.

The police were called and Margerie was briefly taken in for questioning. She told a friend, "They think I've murdered him." And there *were* suspicious circumstances surrounding Lowry's death. The barbiturate tablets he had swallowed were Margerie's and the empty pill bottle was found under clothes in her drawer. No charges were preferred, but some of Lowry's friends thought she could have had a hand in his death. She had the motive, means and opportunity, but there was no Miss Marple in Ripe that week to unravel the mystery.

Margerie's motives were an oft-expressed belief that Malcolm was finished as a writer, her frequent threats to have him committed (once even suggesting he be leucotomized), and her apparent eagerness to go off with the recently-widowed Peter Churchill. As to means, a friend had once caught her feeding pills into Malcolm's open mouth. She claimed they were vitamins which helped him survive next morning's hangover, but could not barbiturates easily have been substituted for

Gordon Bowker

vitamins? The Coroner, however, accepted her story, giving 'misadventure' as his verdict - though she first told friends he had committed suicide for love of her. Mrs Mason backed her at the inquest, saying that Margerie had stayed at her house that night. Interviewed later, however, she said that Margerie had spent the whole night at The White Cottage - which would have given her more opportunity to feed pills to Malcolm than the inquest was led to believe.

Even if innocent of what Malcolm's friends suspected, Margerie's recklessness could have contributed to his death. After all, she could have fed him those barbiturates in mistake for vitamins, or could have left them lying where he could easily get to them. One friend swore that he was incapable of unscrewing a pill bottle, so shaky and uncoordinated were his hands.

Because of drink he was accident-prone - manuscripts were lost, his shack in Canada once burned down. But a strange coincidence might lend credence to the idea of suicide. Lowry was extremely conscious of dates. Every year on the day Paul Fitte died he went into a mental eclipse and often got drunk. The day on which Lowry died was Paul Fitte's birthday.

The 'misadventure' verdict allowed Lowry Christian burial in Ripe churchyard, which a 'suicide' verdict would have prevented. His grave stands behind a low wall in the cemetery to the left of the gateway. Now somewhat neglected and worn, the simple inscription 'Malcolm Lowry 1909 - 1957' is barely readable. Margerie wished to be buried beside him but this proved impossible and when she died in 1988, she was buried at the end of the churchyard overlooking the Downs. Her also weathered headstone bears a line from a song by Strauss, quoted in a Lowry poem evoking the Day of the Dead, when the souls of the departed are reunited: 'Oh, come to me again as once in May.'

When he died, none of Lowry's work was in print in English. Ironically, he had just signed a contract for a US paperback of *Under the Volcano,* and within a few years it was republished here and he was at last recognised in his own country as a writer of stature.

Despite the grim life and the troughs of madness into which he fell, Lowry had a keen sense of self-mocking humour. He wrote his own epitaph, to "Malcolm Lowry, late of the Bowery":

> He lived nightly, and drank daily
> And died playing the ukulele.

Lowry 'liquidate' in British Columbia circa 1952

Torridonian Sandstone

To walk slowly across a landscape, alone
Is to hear the rocks echo and judder,
The wind stream through the cracks
Across the boulder strewn Cambrian quartzite caps.
To climb from a lonely road to a ridge or corrie
Is to see by your feet heather, peat, the tiniest green of Alpine Lady's Mantle.
Touch the rock carved six hundred million years ago
Into buttressed, crazy pinnacled peaks,
At your finger ends weather-worn rounded grains of sand.
Close to your gaze grows the purple of heather, the yellow of Tormentil.
To reach a far distant summit laid down across the wild gap of time
Is to think, long and deep, and to breathe.

Plate 1   Jonathan Harvey. Manuscript Page - from the Second Movement of *Three Sketches, for solo cello* (1988) showing revisions

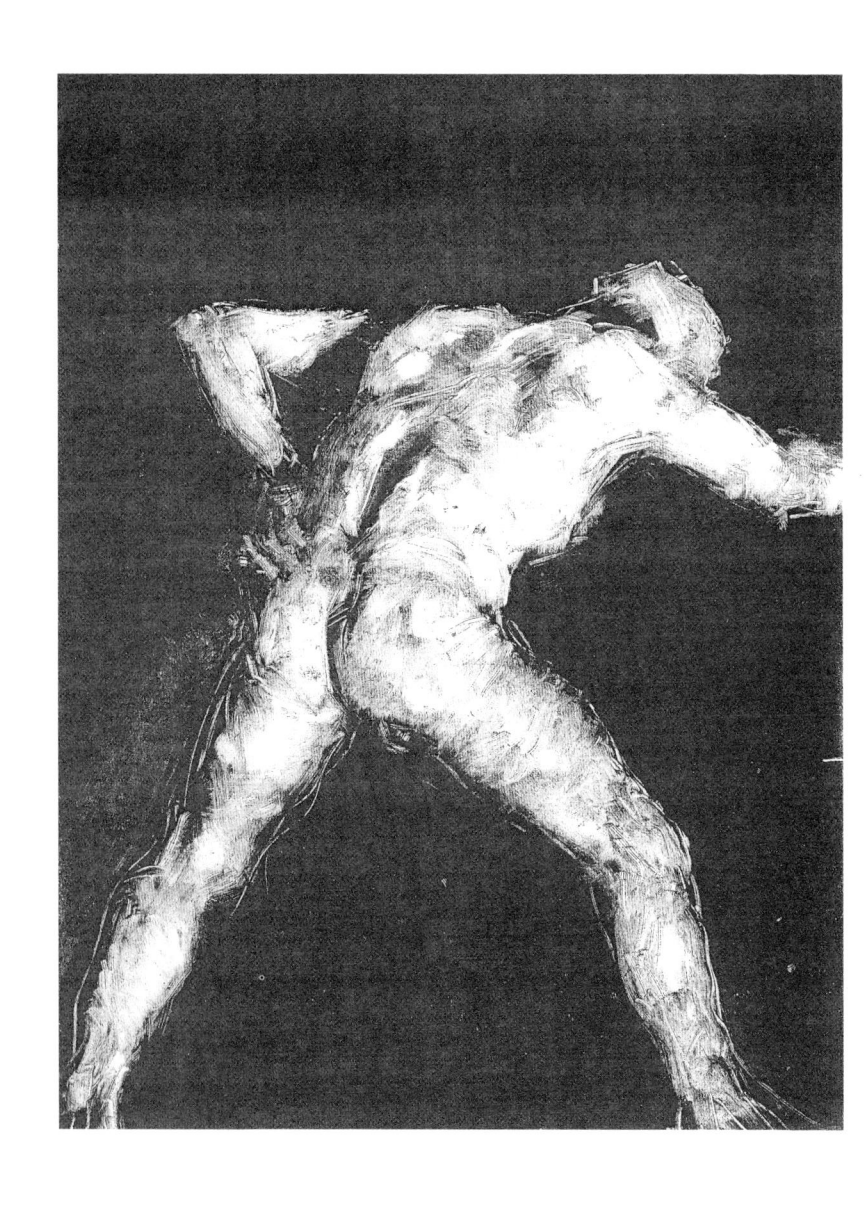

Plate 2   Andy Gammon. Illuminated Man No.1
Monoprint (12 x 9 in.)

Plate 3   Andy Gammon. Illuminated Man No. 5
Monoprint (14 x 10 in.)

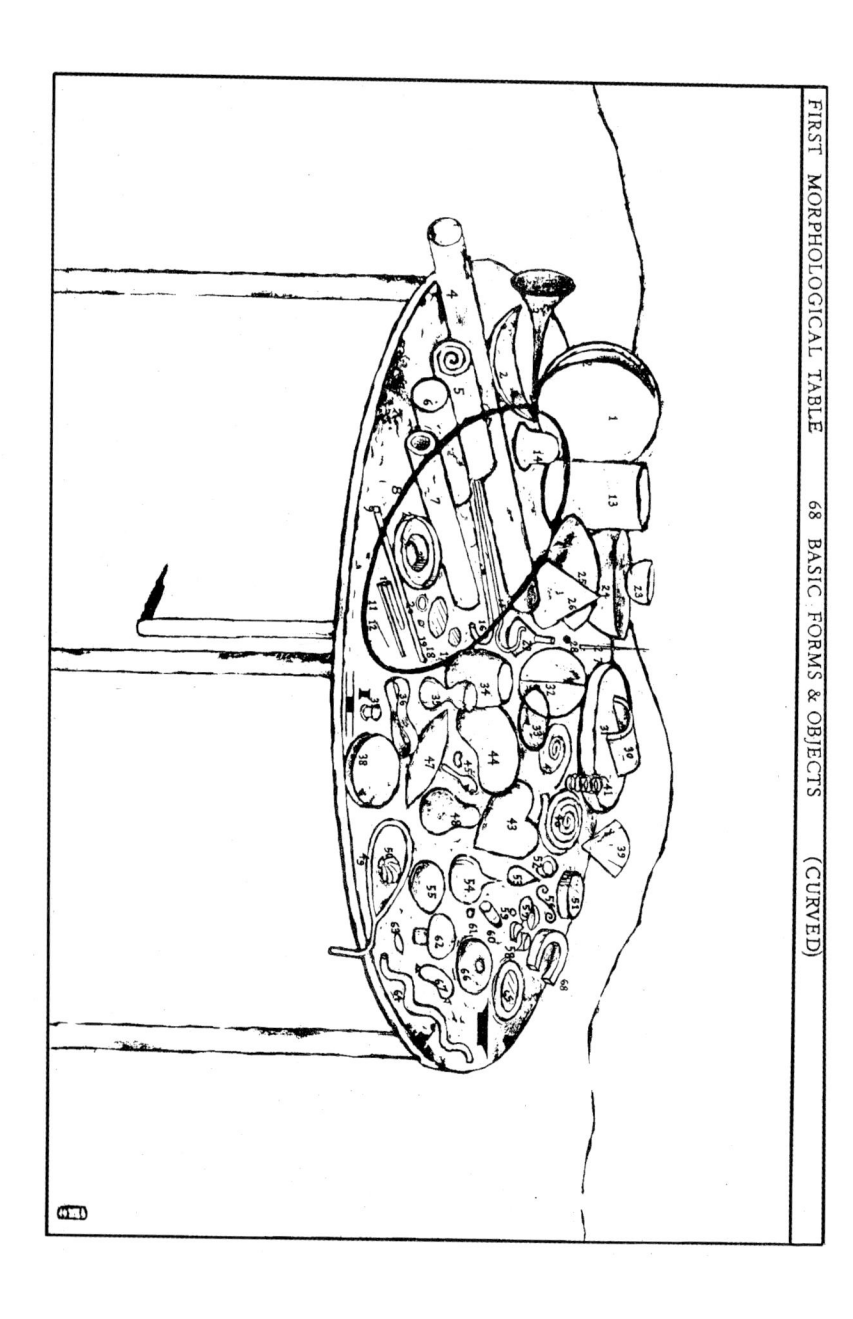

Plate 4   Peter Blegvad. First Morphological Table
68 Basic Forms & Objects (Curved)

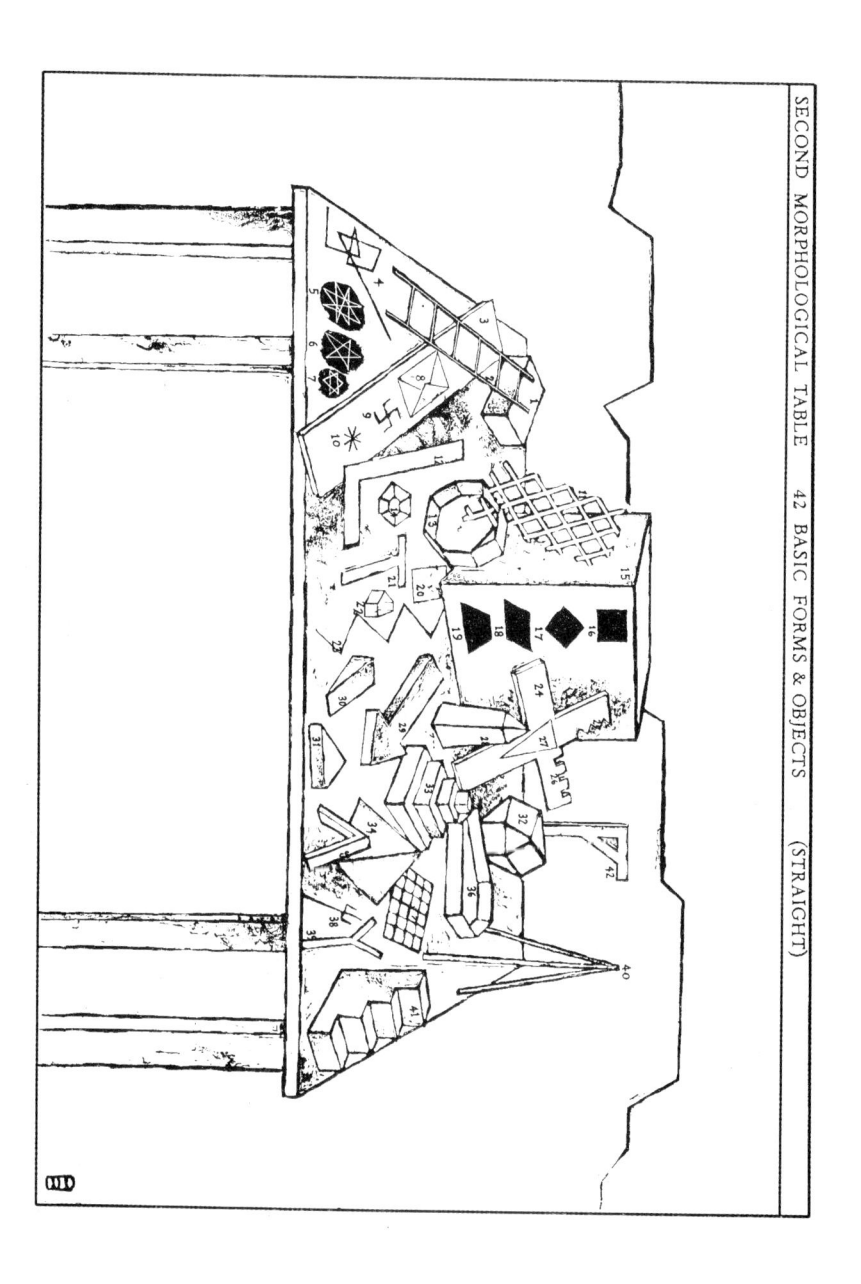

Plate 5   Peter Blegvad: Second Morphological Table
                42 Basic Forms & Objects (Straight)

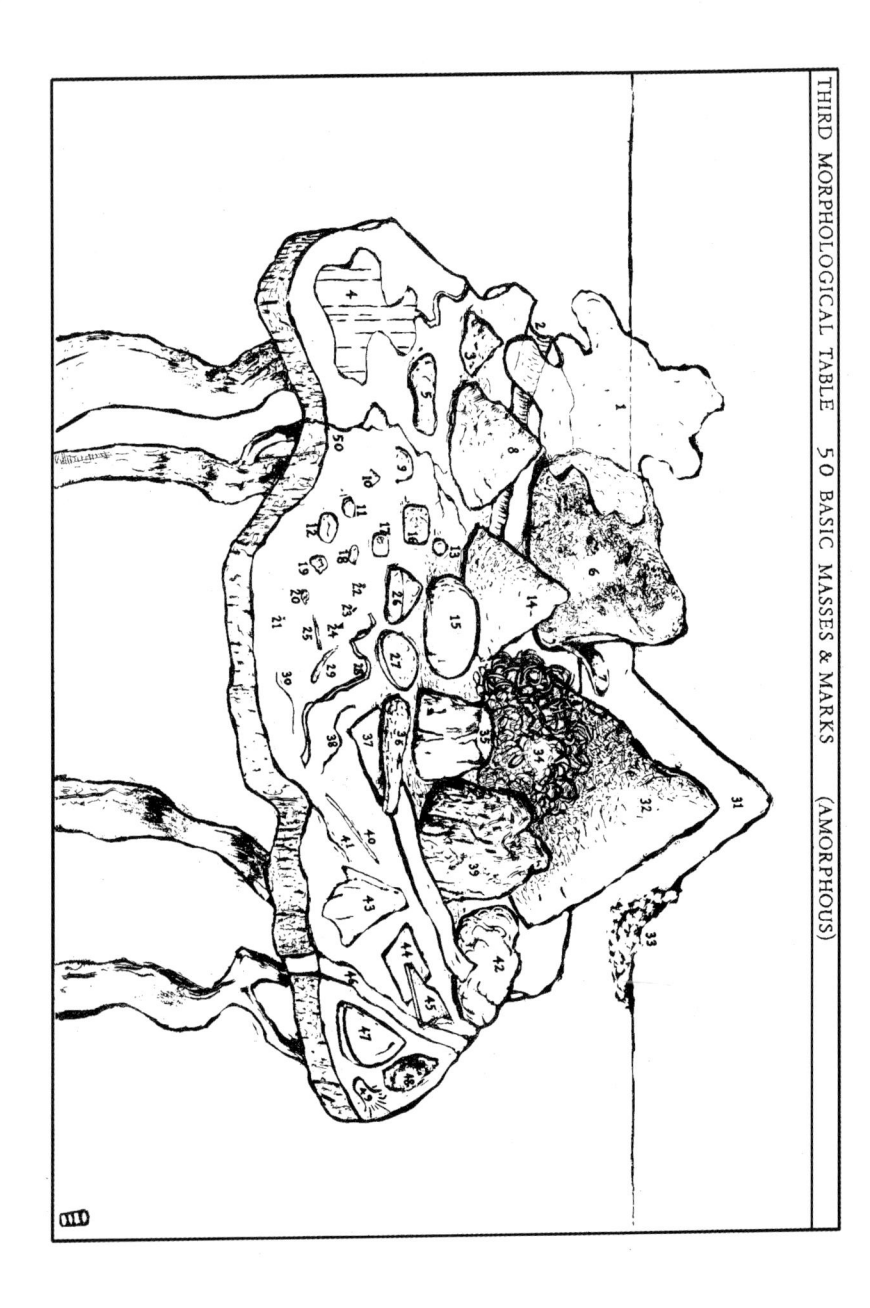

Plate 6   Peter Blegvad. Third Morphological Table
50 Basic Masses & Marks (Amorphous)

KEY

FIRST MORPHOLOGICAL TABLE (CURVED)

1. Sphere, Ball, Globe, Orb
2. Crescent
3. Horn
4. Pillar, Column, Pole, Cylinder
5. Roll
6. Cylinder
7. Tube, Pipe, Hose (if flexible)
8. Hoop (a large Ring)
9. Rod, Wand, Dowel (if wood)
10. Pencil or Stick (as of chalk)
11. Straw (a thin tube)
12. Needle
13. Drum or Cylinder
14. Bell
15. Crook
16. Cane
17. Coin (a small Disk)
18. Disk
19. Grommet (a small Ring)
20. Ring, Terret
21. Circlet
22. Hole
23. Hemisphere (a solid Cup)
24. Hemisphere (a solid Bowl)
25. Elipse
26. Cone
27. Spine, Spike, Tang (a thin Cone)
28. Dot
29. Funnel
30. Arch
31. Wheel
32. Circle (bisected)
33. Oval
34. Barrel, Keg, Tun
35. Hourglass (a verticle Dumbell)
36. Belt or Band
37. Spool w/ cross-
38. Reel } sections
39. Fan
40. Coil
41. Spring, Coil, Gyre, Whorl, Gyre
42. Spiral, Coil, Helix, Whorl, Gyre
43. Heart
44. Kidney
45. Bean (a small Kidney)
46. Spoon, Paddle
47. Cigar
48. Pear
49. Noose
50. Scallop, Shell
51. Puck, Quoit
52. Curl, Loop
53. Teardrop
54. Bulb
55. Egg
56. Scroll
57. Lens (cut in ½ to show convex)
58. Lens (cut in ½ to show concave)
59. Pill
60. Bullet
61. Button
62. Mushroom
63. Almond
64. Serpent
65. Saucer (with cross-section)
66. Donut or Doughnut
67. Sausage
68. Magnet, Horseshoe

SECOND MORPHOLOGICAL TABLE (STRAIGHT)

1. Brick, Box, Rectangle
2. Ladder
3. Plank, Board, Rectangle
4. Line
5. 8-pointed Star
6. Pentagram
7. Seal of Solomon, Star of David
8. Envelope
9. Swastika
10. Asterix
11. Trellis
12. 'L', right-angle
13. Octagon
14. Hexagon
15. Cube
16. Square
17. Diamond
18. Parallelogram
19. Frustrum
20. Sheet, Page, Leaf
21. 'T'
22. Prism
23. Zigzag
24. Cross
25. Saw-tooth
26. Crennelation
27. Pennant, Triangle
28. Obelisk
29. Arrow
30. Wedge
31. Triangle
32.
33. Zigurast
34. Pyramid
35. Chevron, 'A'-Frame
36. Coffin
37. Grid
38. Trident, Fork
39. 'Y', Fork
40. Tripod
41. Staircase
42. Gallows, Gibbet

THIRD MORPHOLOGICAL TABLE (AMORPHOUS)

1. Cloud
2. Ditch, Trench
3. Pile
4. Puddle (with Rill or Runnel)
5. Batch
6. Mass
7. Flap
8. Mound
9. Lump
10. Papule
11. Nugget
12. Blob
13. Bolus
14. Heap
15. Loaf
16. Clod, Clump
17. Plug
18. Wad
19. Glob
20. Morse
21. Crumb
22. Flake
23. Chip
24. Speck
25. Smear
26. Chunk
27. Slice or Flitch
28. Strip
29. Stroke
30. Strand
31. Mountain
32. Hill
33. Talus
34. Tangle
35. Block
36. Cudgel, Club
37. Swathe
38. Thong
39. Hunk
40. Streal
41. Scratch
42. Wedge or Wadge
43. Scrap
44. Swatch
45. Shard
46. Seam
47. Sias
48. Patch
49. Flocculus, Tuft
50. Crack

[MISSING - Nodule & Bump]

Plate 7   Peter Blegvad. Key to Morphological Tables

Plate 8   Paul Taylor. George and Nelson
           Black and White Photograph

What Sort of Music Do You Write?

The year is 1805 and we are in an almost-but-not-quite parallel universe. The aging Haydn has just published an article on his concept of monothematicism in sonata form. The cast of a belated revival of *The Marriage of Figaro* are currently giving workshops in schools and getting children to act out scenes from the opera in a series of previously composed 'improvisations'. Beethoven is giving a pre-concert talk on the *Eroica* symphony, a little hampered by his inability to hear any of the ensuing questions, making the advertised "dialogue with the composer" a slightly one-sided affair....

These three activities are all too familiar ground for composers in the 1990's but would have been inconceivable to the Haydn, Mozart and Beethoven of our own universe. Why do they happen, what are they supposed to do and does anyone actually benefit from them?

The primary expectation from composers was formerly that they should compose, or at any rate, provide music. No-one felt the need for all the explanations and apologies that are now found so necessary. An eminent composer recently observed to me that he actually considered it an essential part of composers' professional training that they should be able to talk and write fluently about their work. I wasn't entirely sure if he was being cynical, realistic or speaking from conviction but he certainly succeeded in starting me thinking about why that which is thought to be so important now was so notably absent in the past.

Today's requirement to talk about what you do rather than just be accepted as doing it is even observable in common conversation. Anyone who has the misfortune to be introduced as a composer comes to expect as a matter of tedious course the inevitable question: "What sort of music do you write?" Most people find it quite impossible to give an adequate response. What do people want to hear? My usual rather lame reply, something along the lines of; "When you've heard a piece of mine then *you* can tell me what sort of music I write" evidently is not acceptable. And yet, if I replied instead*: "I'm into New Complexity, usually micro-tonal with occasional nods in a minimalist direction by way of variation", would that be any more meaningful except to a fellow composer? This is the nub of my problem. The composers of two hundred years ago lived in a culture that supported a common musical language where, in a sense, there was nothing that needed to be explained. In terms of common syntax alone, there was a basic connection between a Beethoven quartet and a Viennese popular song of the time, however great might have been the gulf between the two in profundity or immediate appeal.

---

* *Fairly untruthfully in my case*

Peter Copley

In our time, there abound pieces of western music that might as well have been composed in different planets for all that they have in common and it is not necessary to contrast popular with serious to illustrate the point. Hence all this need to explain. On the one hand there are composers anxious to be understood and rather suspecting that they won't be, and on the other, an audience, lacking the confidence that comes with familiarity, needing elucidation. The fragmented culture that we live in inevitably produces these anxieties in all but the most solipsistic amongst us and I suspect that similar feelings abound among painters and writers. What is questionable is whether the accepted forums for acting out these problems - the technical article, the educational workshop and the pre-concert talk are actually helping anyone.

The technical article is perhaps the least important of my three paradigms. It is usually written for a specialist readership and its chief purpose often appears to be that of self-definition. Once we know what the composer is *for*, or more frequently, *against*, he or she can be slotted, however unjustly, into a convenient pigeon-hole formed by our previous listening experiences. We identify a potential ally or, if in the habit of entering composition competitions, learn to avoid the ones that include the article's author on the jury!

Sadly, composers rarely write well about their own music - few even write well about themselves. Few people, except specialists read Wagner on Wagner nowadays and while Berlioz's memoirs are a literary work of art, it is interesting to note that he largely steered clear from any technical discussion of his music.

This is not to deny the occasional usefulness of such articles, merely to question whether the composers themselves are the best people to write them. Shaw may have been willing to sacrifice half a dozen plays for any one of the prefaces that Shakespeare apparently ought to have written instead, but I suspect that most of us would rather rejoice in the infinite variety of Haydn's sonata forms than lose any one of them for a putative piece of writing explaining them. (It probably would have been on a fairly basic level anyway - if Mozart's comments on his music in letters to his father are anything to go by.)

Besides, throughout music history, theory fairly limped behind practice. Composers had been writing in 'sonata form' for at least half a century before A.B. Marx coined the term in the 1830's One of the more alarming developments of the post-war period was the emergence of theoretical writing that in some cases preceded or even replaced practice. The assiduous student had to learn a new technical vocabulary in every other issue of certain avant garde music journals. There was always the attendant possibility that once this was assimilated, the musical universe would be reinvented again and a new 'year zero' declared. This phenomenon contributed much to the ghettoisation of new music generally and to the unfortunate suspicion on the part of the public that not only was this closed world impenetrable for non-specialists but also that it was no longer worth making the effort.

This sad state of affairs helped to bring about my other two paradigms. The educational workshop and the pre-concert talk are both attempts to bring the composer out of the ghetto and have at least succeeded in proving to a few more people than previously that it *is* possible to be a composer without having to have died more than fifty years ago!

One of the most encouraging developments in school music education has been the requirement for all pupils to engage in some sort of composition as part of their general music training. This has brought many composers into the classroom, often leading workshops in which some of the issues relating to their music are explored in a practical, if often basic context. Clearly, this can benefit the composers as well as the pupils. Placed in a situation where they can assume little or no previous knowledge, the composers can no longer take refuge behind jargon or polemic and are forced to talk and demonstrate by means of concrete example if they are to succeed in communicating at all. While this has often proved to be a valuable and illuminating experience for all concerned, there have been occasions when composition workshops have degenerated into exercises in glossy window-dressing designed to fit current criteria for arts funding. In an ideal world, a composer would be a regular presence in the classroom, but all too often the day to day work is undertaken by someone with little composing experience or, perhaps more importantly, lacking that specific ability to relate the pupils' creative endeavours to current developments in the outside musical world. However, these are early days and it does seem that most composers' experiences visiting schools have been generally positive ones.

Participation in these sorts of events at least has the virtue of bringing composers into contact with a world outside their own rather restricted one. The same could be said of the pre-concert talk - at least in theory. I'm not sure that in practice the benefits are that apparent.

Many composers love pre-concert talks. We are all at our most narcissistic when it comes to explaining what it is all about. However, in the case of a new piece, is there often anything meaningful that can be said before a note has been heard?

The late Hans Keller once gave a series of analytical talks on Beethoven's Quartet Op. 130. What was particularly impressive about them was his complete avoidance of analytical comment on any part of the work that had not been previously heard in the form of a musical example. In other words, his analysis was about a shared experience. In the case of a pre-concert talk, the composer might well know all about the piece but to the listener, he or she is talking about something that does not yet exist; so unless the piece were analysed note by note, the composer can only succeed in directing the audience's attention to a few aspects of the work - inevitably at the expense of others. Alternatively, the composer may choose to be anecdotal in approach which can be entertaining but is ultimately superfluous. Just one composer, in my experience, approached his task with any sense of reality when, on being asked to say something about his piece, stood up, announced that it was in three movements and then sat down again - having misled nobody and prevented applause in the wrong places!

All of these objections to the pre-concert talk would be removed if, instead, there were instigated a *post*-concert talk - preferably in a decent pub. In this situation, there *would* be a shared musical experience as a basis for discussion and there might therefore be some chance of composer and audience making some genuine contact.

It would seem that what with writing explanatory articles, directing workshops and participating in pre-concert talks, the public life of the truly modern composers is in danger of crowding out their one 'raison d'être'. From time to time, we need to remind ourselves of the late Elizabeth Lutyens' stern admonition: "If you are a composer, bloody well sit down and compose!"

Peter Copley

Lol Coxhill

Harbinger's Net

The Visit (1974)

The undercurrent had pulled her all the way down. Down to the slip-stream and below the nets. Beyond the shores to the trackless depths. Down, down to where the whispers called…

The voices coaxed her from the black, imploring her further in. But as she began to succumb to the pull, she heard a voice that was different from the rest. It spoke gently to her from above. It beckoned her back from her sleep.

She opened her eyes and peered over the mountainous folds of the duvet covers. There below the curtains flickers of blue white light danced across the surface of the parquet tiles. She sat up, mesmerised by the spangles of iridescence that drew her from her bed. She threw back the sheets and ran to the burgundy folds that tumbled from the rails so far above her. Was that music outside? Without hesitation she drew back the curtains.

The garden was aglow with a holy light that illuminated the colossal oak at its centre. And above this was an Angel.

She inhaled quickly, hypnotised by the divine creature that shone out above her. Then she noticed that the angel's cassock was caught in the leafy limbs of the tree. He laughed with frustration as he pulled on his gown which stretched taut between him and his captor below. His voice echoed and danced about the garden with the sound of crystal bells.

"Let him go," thought Helen.

In that instant he tugged free his silken trail and flipped awkwardly head over heels into the air. He regained his composure almost immediately, glancing quickly about him as though to check that no-one had observed him, or his exhibition of ungainliness. The angel's voluminous wings beat the night air sending eddies of current through the leaves of the lofty oak. A single feather dropped from his wing and zig-zagged slowly to the earth. The angel watched it fall and met the young girl's gaze. He put his fingers to his lips and whispered through his smile.

"You have seen me. It is a present for you. Share it with those who can also see."

And with this he extended his wings and took to the skies. As he made away the garden lost its glow, and with the sound of fading chimes it returned once more to darkness. All was black, save for the feather that sparkled from the roots of the old tree.

Within minutes the young girl had tip-toed past her mother's room, stolen downstairs and returned with her prize. She pulled the bed clothes over her head and stared into the light that sizzled lazily from the feather.

"It's a present," said Helen with a smile.

Greg Daville

Chapter I. The Storm (1996)

They knew that the storm would hit Southwold that night, well before the crosswinds had joined and begun to howl. They knew it from the year before, and the year before that and the decades that preceded these. As the grey winter sky turned to black the inhabitants hurried home. They counted their children and locked themselves in. Every house was boarded up, every window secured and covered. Sheds were strapped to the earth, boats lashed to the mainland. Trees were felled should they uproot. Animals were brought in from the fields and locked into out buildings, entrances and exits sealed, doors screwed tight. Families huddled together and waited in single rooms. Some gathered food, most did not. All had candles and torches. Some even brought in books or games in the vain hope that they might find some distraction for their families from the incoming storm.

It was not to be; it had already begun. As soon as they heard the low moans of the easterly winds coming in from the North Sea they knew that it was frivolous to consider distraction. Anxious exchanges passed between husbands and wives as squalls came in from the north. They skittered down the street, rising and falling as icy currents joined from the west and south. They channelled themselves along the roads, buffeting the sides of buildings. As they felt their way through the town, a mournful dirge began to build. Tongues of wind extended out, darting down drains and flues, through unsealed windows, up into roofs, joining with whistles and moans from across the town, that rose in chorus as they found points of weakness. The walls of wind battered and sucked; growing in force with a rising wail until they synchronised into a funereal howl.

Within the chaos inhabitants could hear the creaking and splintering of wood, the clattering of metal as it was wrenched painfully away to be swallowed in the screaming vortex. Then above this could be heard the first distant rumbling of thunder. It was coming for the town, galloping across the skies, driving the first of the rains before it across the North Sea. It hit the greens, drumming across the open spaces. The density and speed of the rain increased, whipping across house fronts, pelting down onto roofs. Children clung to mothers and fathers, burying their heads in their chests, their eyes widening to the onslaught about them. And then, as though the rage within the typhoon could not contain itself anymore, a colossal eruption of thunder exploded above the town. Hands instinctively covered hearts as shock waves coursed through nervous systems. Children began to wail at the ferociousness of the giants up above who whipped and stamped and crushed. Driven by an irrepressible anger the winds screed into alley ways and enclosures as thunder blew itself up outside the walls. The sky caved in. It roared down, pulverising all that was exposed, hammering plants and earth to liquid. Sheet lightning detonated in the heavens forcing scythes of white light through uncovered fissures, mocking those cowering within.

The ballistic cacophony discharged demons so drunk with vitriol that they hurled themselves at the sides of the houses in walls of hail. The townsfolk bowed and sobbed from the hammering violation as the sky sizzled and fused with white hot whips. Within, many were fainting, their conscious minds unable to cope with the cyclonic dementia that made the very foundations cry and yawl.

The maelstrom continued raining blow after blow after blow. Finally the thunder and lightning, seemingly exhausted of releasing bellows and bolts, began to pull itself away; the black deed done. From their tiny holes locals listened with fear and hope as they heard it drag itself off the town and back to sea, letting out rumbles of warning and discontent on its way. The winds railed and pitched through the torrent of rain which faded as those few still conscious slipped from exhaustion into sleep, grateful only that they had survived another year's onslaught.

The Keeper of the Net

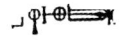

My name is Wyndham Harbinger. I am the Keeper of the Net. The story I am about to tell you began for me over twenty years ago. For others it had begun to unfold before this. It is the story of a curse and the poison and melancholy that has grown from it. And it is about the love and compassion inextricably interwoven with these sadder things. It has not yet ended and even with the gift of foresight granted me by the mystery I still have no sense of its outcome.

I was born in a small town called Southwold on the East coast of England over eighty-six years ago, the son of a postmaster and his wife. I have lived here all of my life. At the time of my childhood it was a small but prosperous fishing community. Every morning we would watch the men put out into the harsh North sea. Then we would emerge and play in what was then only a village; running wild with friends and our young imaginations about the squares and buildings decorated with the masts of ships. We would lose hours careering about the marshes that lay to the west and inevitably find our way down to the beach. It was here that I met the girl who would later be my wife. Years later we married, as did all the locals, in the church of St Edmonds. We enjoyed a harmonious coexistence until she died thirty years later.

In retrospect I suppose that I did not know how lucky I was. I took for granted the beauty of my surroundings, the uncomplicated lifestyle that I led and the love that my wife and I shared with one another. At that time I would have found it difficult, if not impossible to imagine an existence in any way different to the one I had. But of course things do change and shocked as I was at the death of my spouse, I was still less prepared for what was to happen almost immediately after.

Ivy Wyndham had been laid to rest in the grounds of St Edmund's barely three months. I had continued on as though nothing had changed, running the main store and post office of the town. She'd been ill a good year before she passed away and so to some extent I was prepared for it, though I was at a loss as to how to deal with my grief. At best I managed to deny it completely, pushing that deep, deep melancholy somewhere beyond my reach each time it surfaced. To a large extent I had become numb to all about me. With hindsight, I realise that I carried on completely unawares that I was in a state of shock. The reality of it was that my life had become a clockwork version of what had been before. The only solace to break the confused ache I carried about with me was the occasional sense that she was with me. On these rare moments I would feel some of the weight lift and my heart would warm.

Never did Ivy seem more close to me than the day that Madeleine Crow and her daughter Helen entered the Post Office that I had run since my Father retired. She had been bereaved for two years. She had been left on her own to bring up her daughter who was then only six years old. My heart went out to her every time we met. Her husband had drowned on the night of a terrible storm and was found the following morning washed up on the black banks of the River Blythe. It was through her daughter that her spirit found reason to continue, but it was in the church that she sought solace. It was something she never seemed to find. She wore her loss as though she were a martyr to death itself. To this day she has never ceased her grieving and some of the less respectful members of the community still venture that she has lost her sanity. Madeleine Crow has floundered in the sea of a religious mania ever since the death of her spouse.

Her daughter on the other hand, was a bright open child who seemed oblivious to her mother's pain that was so terribly apparent to the rest of us. And so it was that on a sunny June evening they entered my Post office and my sad clockwork world…

The shop bell rang out with a single insistent note as the door opened. I looked up from my paperwork to see Madeleine close the door and lead her daughter to the counter. Helen wore a small red suit. As always, Madelaine was dressed from head to foot in black.

"Good afternoon, Mr Harbinger and how are you?" she enquired in her clipped, educated voice.

"Oh fine, fine, busy as ever you know, lots to do, lots to do."

"Bless you. I know things can't be easy for you at the moment. Helen asked if we could see you. She has a present for you. Haven't you dear?"

She looked down at her daughter with a smile and then almost conspiratorially stared back at me and whispered, "I know everything must seem a trial for you but you know you have friends should you need anything. Anything at all."

She squeezed my arm over the post office counter and continued on, hissing with barely controlled urgency.

"I know how it is to lose a loved one. Anything you need, even if it's someone to talk to, just let me know."

My throat tightened. "Thank you Mrs Crow, it's much appreciated," I replied. I could not control the tears welling up in my eyes.

"There, there," she comforted.

I remember her then, squeezing my arm, her face taut with that martyr's zeal that was so unsettling, and Helen pulling at her mother's skirt.

"Why is Uncle Wyndham crying ?" she asked.

I felt embarrassment mesh with my pain and I forced a smile as Madeleine Crow looked down at her.

"Now Helen where are your manners? Why don't you be a good girl and give Mr. Harbinger his present?"

I recall looking down at her through blurred vision. I opened the counter door and closed it behind me. I picked her up and held her close to me, overcome by her innocence. I closed my eyes and hugged her more.

"Look what I got!" she exclaimed

I sat her down on the counter top and wiped my eyes as she fumbled excitedly with her toy handbag.

"Pay no notice," her mother whispered, "I tried to get her to throw it away but she insisted on bringing it here to give to you."

Memory is a strange thing. We drag it out like an old keepsake stored on a dusty shelf and re-examine it. Then we polish it up a bit, perhaps even adding a coat of paint before sharing it with ourselves or with our friends. Years later, when we want to do the same again, we take it down from the shelf quite forgetting that we have added to it each time it has been recalled. We just presume that this layer of paint was always on it. So more often than not, our memories are merely memories of memories and not of the original events. Consequently they grow and change of their own accord unnoticed by us, reflecting little of the original event or the truth. But on very rare occasions some things can happen that are so startling, so intense in their original form that they burn themselves into our mind's eye deep enough to become absolute. And when these memories are recalled they can only appear as they were originally perceived; the moment forever virgin, always shocking.

This was such a moment. I recall with absolute clarity Helen's beaming face and the excitement with which she announced that she had brought me a gift. I remember Madeleine turning her eyes to the ceiling and raising her eyebrows as if to say 'what a fuss, just humour her' and me turning back to the little girl who was fumbling to open her purse. She tugged at the plastic clasp until it finally unlocked. The bag opened and in that split second an intense light burst from the container and illuminated the entire room. The sunlight beaming at angles through the store window died under the unearthly blue luminescence that painted itself into every corner and onto every surface. In panic I looked to her mother, but it was plain to see by her indifferent expression that she was not experiencing the same thing.

Completely flabbergasted I returned my attention to Helen who was now holding in her hand whatever had been in the bag. It was impossible to see what it actually was as the light fused my vision with the lambence of burning mercury. I shot a glance at Madeleine, but she seemed in another world, smiling thinly down at Helen with feigned interest.

"But what is it?" I stammered to her daughter, trying in vain to focus on what she held.

"Its an angel's feather," she said with a smile.

My hands shook as I took the fiery thing from her. I held it by the stem, speechless at its phosphorescent beauty. It hummed with light. Never had I seen something, anything, so shockingly beautiful. I shielded my eyes with my other hand. In that moment, as though my senses had suddenly become illuminated by the dancing incandescence, I realised that I was part of a world that was fantastically bigger and infinitely more mysterious than I had ever realised.

"But its beautiful!" I cried.

"I know," said Helen matter of factly. "It's an angel's feather."

I started as Madeleine announced that Helen should stop pestering me as it was time for them to leave. I recall her lifting her off the counter and apologising for her over enthusiastic daughter. She wished that God be with me and promised to drop by the next day as she dragged a very proud looking six year old girl out of the shop.

I managed to lock the door behind them and holding the feather at arms length, stumbled to the back room so as to conceal the light from passers-by. I charged into the room and trying to catch my breath laid it delicately on the old oak writing desk that had once been my father's. The feather zinged and hummed with an energy beyond my ken. The back room was then near empty save for a few old boxes and the desk. It was damp and had remained disused for many years, but now its dark corners full of spider's web and junk resonated with this triumphant light. I drew up a chair and utterly mesmerised simply stared; for how long I am not completely sure, it could have been for hours. But as I did images from my childhood began to dance in front of me. They mingled in crystalline profusion with other pictures from my life. They splintered and crashed into one another like waves: suddenly I was running along the shore with the other children, then I was spinning around with my Ivy on the day of our wedding. Fishermen dragged in their haul and rising nets, as the sea pounded against the eastern shores. Villagers scurried through through the years, growing and building houses, giving birth to their families who in turn had children as Ivy and I looked on; a sadness in her green eyes until finally, once again, she lay before me on her death bed, her face now serene.

The light began to fade and before I knew it I had fled sobbing from that room and my home down to the sea. For the first time since Ivy had died I could no longer hold back the pain. It roared out in staccato sobs. The grief welled up and hacked its way out of my bones, coursing out until I thought I would break. It continued on and on until at last I was still; a silent wreck on the beach, oblivious to the tides and the stars that peeped through the evening mist. I remained still as the they crept across the vastness of the black sky until finally I came to my senses; shivering, yet calm.

After the Storm

Eliot heaved back the big door; its metal wheels squealing against the metal runners. With a grunt he slid it aside. A pale rectangle of light fell onto the artist's wiry frame and into the barn's interior behind him. His thick gold mane was held in place by a length of red paisley silk. Blonde sideburns framed his gaunt face from which shone a pair of piercing blue eyes. He stepped out onto the concrete patio that led down to the landing bay by the river. He winced from the brightness before him. The marshes glistened against the pale winter sun and there beyond the bogs also glistening, was Southwold. From this distance, the patchwork town-scape looked normal enough, but he knew that after the storm last night only destruction could lay across the way; possibly injury, perhaps even death. He shuddered in the early morning air which bit through his silk nightshirt. From here the tops of the buildings glistened unnaturally. He shivered.

"I will not go there to day!" he hissed to himself, lighting a cigarette.

A grunting noise distracted him and he turned to see the other artist emerge from the boat shed that was their home. Scull dragged an all too small t-shirt over his colossal torso. He stumbled out like a blinded giant, until his vast close-shaven head emerged through the neck of the shirt.

"Morning," he mumbled, opening his eyes.

Eliot ignored him and returned his gaze to the town. There was something altogether unsettling about the light on the buildings. The weak morning sunlight adhered to the roofs in globs like the surface of a crude oil painting. It repulsed him.

"Ready for work?" Scull nodded towards the town in a cheery, earthy sort of way that instantly irritated Eliot.

"No, I'm not," he replied curtly. "You will be going in without me this morning. Today I'm to start my masterpiece. It's going to be an ongoing conceptual work of such profundity that it will flood the world of contemporary art with resonant cultural waves."

Scull's block-like jaw dropped open.

"But what about all the work that will need doing? What about the people who need help?"

"Sod the people and sod the town! I've got more important things to do than mop up after a little rain. I'll start my own work and escort you in tomorrow. Still, before this, breakfast. And it's your turn to make it."

"But…" mouthed Scull in exasperation.

"No arguments," said Eliot, making his way back into the boat shed with a dismissive wave. "I did it yesterday. A bacon sandwich will do nicely thank you. I'm going for a shower." He disappeared into the heart of the building and without looking around shouted, "And cut off the fat before you cook it!"

"Idiot," sighed Scull with a shake of his head.

He spent the whole morning trying to convince an ill-tempered Eliot to accompany him to the town. The damage caused by the storm guaranteed them at least two months paid labour. As artists the work was invaluable to them both. Scull would work through the early winter and with the money he saved could then concentrate all his efforts on his sculpture.

Every year the storm acted as a watershed for the occupants of the town who would literally rebuild their lives. Scull enjoyed this sense of starting anew. Unfortunately it seemed to have engendered in Eliot the need to make new art. Eliot was insistent; apparently he felt inspired. He could not and would not go into Southwold. He simply had to begin his own work.

Scull sighed to himself as he watched the door slam behind his flat-mate and listened as Eliot marched aggressively to his studio above. Scull stood up and pushed through the kitchen door. A partitioned bedroom opened up onto his workshop. The whole building had originally served to store and service boats. Its big open spaces were perfect as studios.

Once in the bedroom, Scull prepared himself for the day ahead. He pulled on a fisherman's roll-neck pullover and tugged steel toe-capped boots onto his size twelve feet. He wrapped a huge leather belt of tools about his waist and went into the workshop. A small boxer pup shuddering impatiently in his wicker basket could contain his excitement no more and propelled himself across the concrete floor. He slipped and regained balance, slipped again then launched himself with a yelp at Scull.

"Alright Bosch?" said Scull, his thick Liverpudlian drawl belying the affection he had for the dog. Every syllable he uttered had a way of sounding like a moan. He scooped the dog up in one hand, placed a kiss on his head then returned him to the floor.

"Well mate, it looks like it's just us two today."

He took his leather biker's jacket from the peg on the back of the door and pulled it on. Painted in gold capitals on its back was the declaration 'Verdi is God'. He crouched slightly to check his reflection in the mirror on the shelf next to the tool rack. He was good looking in such a plain way that he was almost ugly. His big square head looked as though it were hewn from oak.

His grey green eyes sank under a bar of bone that was his forehead, above which an economic flat-top haircut sprang to attention from his cranium. He ran a huge fist of fingers quickly through his dark hair.

"That's alright," he sighed as though trying to reassure himself, then picking up a colossal tool kit looked down at the dog shivering with excitement.

"Let's go lad."

Bosch wagged his tail maniacally and scampered after Scull to the lorry parked at the back of the studio. The winter winds coming up from the River Blythe bit into his face. He opened the cab door, dropped the pup onto the passenger seat then pulled himself in. He turned the key and the truck's engine exploded into life. The cassette player clicked on and Verdi's 'Requiem' blared from the speakers. Scull began to sing along in his enthusiastic tenor voice, perfectly out of key. The lorry growled and hissed as it trundled by the hundreds of boats moored alongside the Blythe. The truck bumped over the estuary bridge, Sculls voice increasing in volume. Over the brim lay the marshes. Acres of bog stretched out to the perimeters of Southwold and the sea beyond the town. Between the marsh vegetation pockets of flood water glistened with a pale lemon luminescence.

Scull stopped singing. "My God…" he gasped.

The entire landscape was peppered with black fish. They hung from the scrub and littered the grass flats in thousands. He pulled the lorry up onto the verge and leapt from the cab, slamming the door behind him. Hundreds of shining black sea-creatures were skewered onto the hawthorn bushes that lay along the roadside. Hundreds more were scattered along the grass. He approached the bushes slowly. He gazed down at one of the fish and prodded it with his foot. It was dead, they were all dead. He bent on his haunches and picked one up in his gloved hands by the tail. He did not recognise the species. It measured six inches from tail to head. Its black scales were coated in a film of blue jelly. Its large mouth hung open as if in agony. Its eye was a huge glop of black blindness. Scull dropped it to the ground with distaste.

"Jesus."

Bosch whined from the truck. Scull hauled himself back into the lorry and started it up. His eyes moved from across the scrubland to Southwold. Shoals of land-bound fish glittered ominously under the winter sky.

"Alright boy," he whispered, "Let's see what's happened in town…"

~

The dwarf watched the young red haired woman labouring away at the back of the big house. From here her pale skin seemed to shine, reflecting back the cold afternoon light. Helen put down the wheelbarrow and waved.

"Morning, Mrs Fibonnaci."

Mrs Fibonnaci hobbled over towards Helen.

"Morning love, cleared your garden yet?"

"Yes. I've been at it since six. This is the last barrow load and I'm done."

Mrs Fibonnaci stared up at the pile of fish with distaste.

"Well at least they don't smell. They're the oddest thing I've ever seen. Don't make sense, fish not smelling. And look at the colour…" She fidgeted uncomfortably. "I don't want to sound pessimistic but the storm seems to get worse every year."

"I agree," sighed Helen. "Have you had much damage to your place?"

"Not too bad, but we haven't cleared up yet. I must be off. Don't want John moaning at me for the rest of the day. See you later dear."

"See you."

Helen watched the tiny woman cross the green and disappear into the crowds of people working on the town. She tugged at the barrow and led it along the side of the house to the back garden where a mountain of fish peeked up at the sky. She leant on the garden path and gazed up to the bedroom. Her mother was walking back and forth, worry beads in hand, waiting for the arrival of the vicar. Helen's eyes drifted to the colossal oak. It sighed and swished as the winter wind combed through its branches and leaves. She absent-mindedly took off her gloves and tossed them to the barrow.

Her eyes returned to the oak. The old tree seemed comforting somehow. She had gazed upon its gnarled, solid, features since she was a child. She closed her eyes and let images waft into her mind. A little girl scampered through vast rooms… her bedroom …the huge brass bed in lace, the vast french windows that framed the oak outside.

"Need any help?"

She snapped out of her reverie with a jolt. It was Scull.

"No thank you kind sir." replied Helen. "But perhaps the gentleman would like some tea?"

"Lovely," he replied, rubbing his hands together. He followed her through the back door and into the kitchen. She filled the kettle and left it on the Aga, pointing to a chair and motioning Scull to sit.

"You've been busy I see," said Scull nodding towards the fish outside.

"I bet you have as well. There must be a lot of work to do in the town."

She sat down and taking out a packet of tobacco began rolling a cigarette.

"And where is his highness this morning?"

Scull raised his eyebrows in consternation. He spoke in a low voice, the words coming out slowly as if he had to consider each one before saying them.

"Oh he's begun another masterpiece… You know, we need this great cultural triumph… this morning!" He jabbed at the air with his finger, unable to disguise his frustration. "The one day of the year Eliot and me are guaranteed to get loads of work!"

Helen laughed and poured boiling water into the pot.

"A little something to perk up your jasmine?"

She grinned as she pulled out a bottle of Jamesons from the open cupboard.

"That'll do nicely," smiled Scull, rolling a cigarette from Helen's tobacco. "I'm dead," he sighed. "I've been all round town and there's enough work to keep us going for three months. The Wood's place has been nearly flattened and Grace's roof caved in." He dragged on the rolly. "It's only old man Harbinger who seems to have missed the storm. Just like last year and the one before that. I sometimes think he's charmed."

"Oh he is," said Helen matter of factly, pouring a shot of whiskey into each mug of tea.

"Oh not that again. I'm amazed at you believing all that stuff. It gives me the willies. Leave well alone, that's what I say."

"Rational man speaks with superstitious tongue," mocked Helen.

"Well…" intoned Scull gruffly. "It's simple, what you see is what you get. That's what I say."

"Like fish falling from the heavens…" said Helen with a grin.

"Well, I dunno." A frown of confusion formed itself on his brow. He rubbed his hair uneasily. She smiled affectionately back at him.

"Believe what you believe, whatever makes you happy."

They spent awhile talking about Scull's day and Helen's experience of the storm. She looked at the wall clock. "Right, I'm going to have to ask you to leave. I've got to clear the front of the house and the vicar's coming over to see Mum."

"Ok" he drawled.

He downed the last of his tea and stood up. Helen went over to him and hugged him.

"Listen, tell that idiot friend of yours that you're both invited to come round for a meal. The Krankenman has done a special wine to celebrate the storm's passing. Bring Eliot round and we can all get terribly ill together."

"Sounds good to me,"

She rose on her tiptoes and kissed him on the cheek. "See you later."

She followed him out to the back garden. He hauled himself into the lorry cab and was immediately put upon by a slobbering, over enthusiastic pup.

~

Mr Harbinger finished inspecting the post office and his living quarters and noted in his book that there was no damage to be seen. Not without a little guilt, as he took in the damage and rectification going on all about him in the rest of the town. He left his house and spent a few hours helping the townsfolk; stacking roof tiles, collecting fish, consoling those too old to bear the brunt of yet another storm.

Mrs Tolley had wiped away the tears with a small handkerchief and looked up at the silver haired man, caught in the benevolent gaze of his brown eyes.

"I'm sorry Mr H," she sighed. "Maybe I'm getting old, but it seems such an effort to keep this place up. It's not just the storm, it's this…" She let her hands indicate the damaged porch. "I sometimes wonder what I have to live for." Her shoulders began to shake and she began to sob.

"Now, now Rose," said Harbinger squeezing her shoulder. "We'll get this fixed soon enough and you know I'm always here when you need me don't you?"

He grasped her arm and standing a pace back gazed into her eyes.

She smiled through the tears and quietly replied, "Yes. I'm sorry Wyndham."

"Don't be silly. I'll let Scull know that you're house is on the top of the list for repairs. Ok?"

"Alright." she sighed. She dried her eyes and replaced the handkerchief in her sleeve.

"Good. Now I'll pop up later as soon as I've been round the rest of the town. Alright?"

"Yes. Thank you."

"Ok."

"See you later Mr H."

As he got to the garden gate he stopped and turned around to face her. "Rose?"

"Yes, Mr Harbinger?"

"Here's something that might make you happy. I do believe your Becky's got some good news for you."

"Has she? Are you sure?" She looked at him excitedly. "What exactly?"

"Best ask her. It's just a feeling I have…" He winked at her and waved, then continued down the street. The pavements and gardens buzzed with activity as the inhabitants of Southwold laboured to clear and rebuild their homes.

~

Harbinger sat at a small roll-top desk and finished another entry in his log. He scrawled with a quill: Dulcett, Becky. Second daughter of Tolley, Rose. He then wrote Dulcett, Debby. To arrive 8 months, 7 days hence. He closed the log and copied the text onto the back of a brown envelope. He replaced the quill then stood up, feeling the bottom of his back as he stretched. He looked about the room. Each of the four walls was covered with hundreds of snippets of paper, all covered with his tiny, neat hand writing. They joined one another in a system of tape, pins and lengths of string.

"Now let's see…" he whispered to himself.

He peered over his glasses. He walked over to the far corner and ran his forefinger slowly down a strip of gaffer tape that rose from the skirting board to the ceiling. Dates were scrawled along its length. He let his finger follow it down then ran it across to a small sub-section with the name 'Tolley' inscribed on a dog eared piece of tape. Beneath this were the names of all her relatives. From here a thin wire hung away from the wall. On the end of the wire was a tiny card box. Taped over its corner was the word Deborah. He folded the envelope in half and inserted it into the box.

"There." He smiled and stood back, taking in the chaos of labels, wires and strings that not only covered the walls but also hung from the ceiling.

"Hmm I'm going to have to get an assistant if I'm going to keep this up…" he mused. He stepped up to the centre of the main wall, and let his finger glide slowly over a yellowed paper sellotaped onto it. It read *Helen Crow*. His fingers caressed a small piece of string that went from under the tape, six inches across to another tag which bore the name *Eliot Mercurius (Artist)*. His finger went from this to the next, on which was written *Randolph Scullion (Artist)*. A long horn blasted briefly outside, the sound of Mozart emanating from beyond.

"That'll be Mr Scullion now I should think."

He shuffled to the door, had one last brief look at the room. He shut the door and locked it. At the front of his house was the post office and general store. He got to the counter as Scull sauntered in through the front door.

"Well, well, well. Hello Scull."

"Afternoon, Mr H," mumbled Scull, running his hand through his hair. "Just thought I'd pop by before I got home. See if there's any jobs for me".

"Well, now you should mention it, Mrs Tolley's having a problem with her porch."

"Ok. I'll look in first thing tomorrow."

"Now, I know how busy you have been, but I'm sure she would appreciate it all the more if you could look at it today." His eyes smiled over his glasses

Scull looked back silently.

"It's reassurance more than anything else you see…" He swung the counter top back on its hinges and came into the shop. He could see the tiredness in Scull's eyes. "She mentioned something about a large bag of scraps that might be appreciated by a growing hound."

Scull sighed.

"And you might like this." He went over to the rack of cassettes. He picked one out and handed him one.

"Country and Western?" Scull frowned.

"Only joking, of course" smiled Harbinger. He replaced the cassette in the rack and pulled out another from his overall pocket. "I recorded it from the radio a few nights ago. It's Bach's cello solos. Very good. Have you got them?" His eyebrows arched slightly.

"No." Scull flustered. "Brilliant." He smiled. "Thanks Mr H. I'll pop over and see her now."

"Oh good. She will be pleased."

Scull stumbled awkwardly out of the shop. The lorry boomed into life, Scull waved as he pulled off. Choral music exploded from the cab. Harbinger smiled and closed the door.

~

Eliot looked out and across at the flat lands. A fog had begun to build about the town's parameters. He watched, enchanted as the mist grew higher and higher, forming a veil which continued to extend up, covering first the outer fields, then the small cottages. It rose until the lighthouse, which was the tallest building in town, became hidden from view. The skirt of fog extended twice the height of the lighthouse, three times and more, until it began to mushroom, slowly forming what looked like the shape of an old man. From folded arms grew a torso and eventually a cowled head.

"It's back" he mused, trying to ignore the shiver that scurried across his spine. He pulled out a small, black note book from his Harris Tweed jacket and scrawled something in its pages with an antique Parker pen. He returned the book to his pocket. As he did, something dropped from its pages. A small photograph of Helen. He pulled out a pair of glasses from his breast pocket and studied it. In the picture she was raising a pint of ale to the camera, her head half thrown back in laughter. She wore a pullover of Scull's which was much too large for her. Her red hair was pulled loosely back. He smiled to himself and returned the photo between the leaves of the book. His eyes returned to the landscape. The colossal figure was now so dense that it looked as though it could have been made from slate; if it were not for the almost imperceptible glow that flickered on and off from its centre and the lighthouse within. A slight melancholia began to grow in the pit of his stomach and moved slowly to his heart.

Something changed in his field of vision. He looked across to the cloaked town as a tiny black speck burst from the foot of the sea fret wall. The distant roar of Sculls's lorry was reduced to a hum that carried across the marshes. It careered across the marshland. It vanished behind hedge rows that lined the tiny lanes, reappearing occasionally at break neck speed. He followed it to where he thought it was until it emerged at a small cross roads. He could hear the hiss and crack of gears changing down, then the roar of acceleration as it got closer. Just above the rattle and grind of the engine, the sound of Verdi's Requiem dispersed into the winter mist. He breathed in the evening cold, then fumbling in his waist coat pocket pulled out a small bakelite case. He pulled back the narrow door on its top. A cigarette was gently ejected. He drew it out with his lips and lay back on the damp grass.

"Oh Helen" he sighed, with a tiredness in his voice.

He lit the cigarette and looked up at the darkening sky, the first stars appearing. He thought of her in that old pullover, pulling it gently over her head and shoulders, kissing her belly, then her breasts, pulling her on top of him and kissing her neck. He hugged her, and for the first time realised that up until this point in his life, something had been missing. He could almost see the final piece of jigsaw falling into place and was flooded with warmth. He kissed her back, as they watched the mist come in by the estuary. Later on Scull managed to fall into it, all three crawling back to the studio, soaked, drunk and happy.

Something changed. A distant noise became a wild scampering. Something was coming from across the grass. He flushed hot and cold and threw himself over. Before he could get up Bosch was at him, licking his face madly.

"You mutt!" he cried with relish, pulling the dog over and tickling his chest. "You little mutt" he laughed. "You scared me to death." He grabbed the dogs paws and rubbed his exposed belly furiously. "I'll teach you! I'll teach you!" He growled at the pup's jaws. Scull appeared, towering above the two. He held a card box under his arm.

"Alright?" asked Scull.

"Yeah. How was it in town?"

Scull squatted next to the dog and rubbed his head. "Oh you know, hard work…"

"Hmm. Sorry, I simply couldn't have gone in today. I'll come in tomorrow." Then looking at Bosch said, "Won't I boy? Won't I boy".

Scull was frowning.

"What's wrong?" Eliot sat up

"Well you know… It's what I said before. I want him to be a one man dog. Only I should stroke him if he's going to learn."

Eliot deliberately pawed at the boxer. "One man dog. One man dog! Who's a one man dog then hey?!"

"Eliot." Scull asserted, gently pushing him away. Eliot sat up.

"Oh for God's sake Scull. The animal's too soft to be nice to one person." He stroked him again "Aren't you boy? Aren't you?"

Bosch laid on his back, his forelegs cocked at right angles, tail twitching madly.

"See many people in town?" enquired Eliot, offering Scull a cigarette.

"Yep. And Mrs Tolley kindly donated this bottle of her homemade nettle wine."

"Excellent" Eliot rubbed his hands together.

"Actually she gave me a crate." smiled Scull, nodding down at the box.

"Lovely. Well open her up. You can never keep a good wine waiting. Or a bad one come to that."

Scull extracted a Swiss Army knife from his leather jacket and de-corked it. He took a slug "A little harsh" he mimicked Eliot " But wine nonetheless"

"Excellent! Here, here!"

Three bottles later their raucous hollering could be heard across the night sky, interspersed by the occasional bark.

Further onto the flats the colossal figure made of fret continued its vigil over the tiny town.

The Astrologer and the Ant

"God?"
Said the astrologer
"I don't believe in God"
I wanted to demolish her
It really boiled my blood
Believing there is meaning
In the movement of a star
While belief in something bigger
Means you take belief too far

And then I thought of Becky who
When she was only four
Heard Lucy (thirty three) say she
Believed in God no more
Becky said, "Well tell me then
Who made the sun and sea?
Who made the moon? Who made the stars?
The buffalo? The bee?

Who made the wind? The world? The rain?
Who made the sand and sky?"
"Natural phenomena"
Was Lucy's faint reply

And once I saw a frantic ant
In panic stricken state
My hand immense and monstrous
Brushed it from a picnic plate
It once believed in breadcrumbs
And of waging ant-like war
But the doors of it's perception now
Are wider than before

And then I thought of Harry who
Was moved by mystery
Performing as a shepherd
In his first nativity

"And do you see the baby Jesus?"
Harry staggered back
Then said with wide-eyed wonder
"How on earth did you know that?"

Children have no problem with
Belief in deities
Every day a bigger being
Brings them to their knees
And ants are well aware of things
They cannot comprehend
A move from something massive
Might well bring about their end

And me I think the frantic ant
In panic stricken state
The child who asks a question
In a way that grown-ups hate
The flower that lifts its head towards
Whoever holds the hose
The bee that flies unerringly
Towards the distant rose

All of these and more of these
I cite as evidence
Of that which is most holy:
Intelligence

And if there is intelligence
It cannot be confined
There may well be intelligence
Of universal size
Or maybe not. But if there is
And ant-like I decide
If it's big it must be dangerous
Let's run away and hide

Then I have accomplished what?

Intelligence denied.

John Dowie

It's September. Zonah[1] has started school. The wind blows that cheap and nasty netting in from the window. Anyway I will move. It flicks across the page. I'm not sitting comfortably (on a Warre's Vintage Port[2] box) and my back aches. Instead I'll go to the kitchen. Endure the washing cycle. Find a pen that does not blur the image. And write what possibly, will be, my last serious piece for two years. Chay[3] will wake up soon. Life is interruptions. I'll hear Sonay Saato's quiet music [4] audibly rather than the odd note. Things are less than conducive. Writers don't fear time, in headphones, knowing a bottle will be called for soon. I keep thinking of hunger.

Introduction to Mythologies/Nine Men's Morris/ A period of my life in August 1997

Synopses:

Komitas
a film about a specific time in Armenia and the consequences for one man in particular, namely 1915, composition, silence, a film deeply rooted in culture.

Lost Highway
a film about two people, the man who can transmogrify into another person, the woman who can be another person. Nothing worthy occurs because this film is rooted, not deeply, in fantasy.

The Sacrifice
a film about a man who sacrifices. And a postman who is enigmatic. Operates on many levels, not least fantasy.

1. Komitas
a) Film reviewers.
Where I read or heard this I don't know, but it still sticks in my mind. Somewhere in Soho red-eyed box-office film reviewers sit in early morning gloom to preview the oncoming films.

---

1. **Zonah**. *Zonah Michelle Graham - b. 9.6.93. Named after the Zone in Stalker. Prefers the name Rosie herself.*
2. **Warre's Vintage Port**. *A renowned drink. Not religious drinking.*
3. **Chay**. *Chay Yefim Graham - b. 23.9.96. Middle name comes from The Commissar, accurate details of which I haven't got here, but research would reveal. Yefim is the man of great tolerance.*
4. **Sonay Saato**. *A cassette tape has one piece of his or hers recorded off Radio 3. The music is sparse, quiet, but not devotional.*

The room, for it is not a cinema, is filled with smoke and there are bags under their smog eyes. Perhaps it's something I dreamt, like a chocolate box cover. Could you imagine, say, Pauline Kael's [5] bag-eyed features leaping out Wurlitzer [6] style from Cadbury's Milk Tray [7]. Whose voice was this myth, this 10am smoke, sparse. With what narrowing do we receive these inessential reviews? The smoke lingers and the credits roll? What makes you see a film? Or write a story? Up they all get, long, long before the credits roll. A real audience, this, having sat through Lost Highway. From 10am smoke, drink, blur to evening, late night, even all night audience. Buffs, cinéastes, old, young, queer, straight, black, white; order, deliberate. The reviewer is a freak. It's a freak job, suitable only for making legends. Still, as I said, it could have been a dream and it might not have been Soho.

b) Watching one film takes me several nights indoors on a portable. I've got to contend with masses of horrible things, one of which is so horrible I'm stunned and shocked for several days. The list is fairly usual. Externalities like neighbours drilling, the adverts, (fasted forward can actually be worse), sound quality, cars…. it's my children's room and they leave their dreams and mythologies lying on the ground, on shelves above. Between me and the screen is no oasis, it's a noir of junk. The horrendous incident happened ON TOP of all these things I was contending with… (and here I divert…) I had a whole listing of Komitas intertitles (all 14) but I've lost the paper on which I jotted them. I consider recollecting them. To collect again. I cannot recollect them. How important is memory? My memory remembers the horrendous very well. I forget the rewinding to collect intertitles. I remember bits of the film. About one third through, Trake [8] comes home, immediately hits switch mode, first the light, then the set and I'm plunged into a documentary, a film medium of colossal potential, like film itself, about the Osmonds [9].

---

5. **Pauline Kael**. *Critic of film whom I've never read. Born, definitely.*
6. **Wurlitzer**. *Who is or was he or she?*
7. **Cadbury's Milk Tray**. *A favourite, heavily advertised brand of assorted chocolates, probably made at Keynsham.*
8. **Trake**. *Tracey Dawn Graham, née Cartwright - b. 7.2.61. Trake means conscientious interrupter of the holy and the profane.*
9. **The Osmonds**. *Donny, Jay, Merrell (poss)Wayne, Alan, Marie, Jimmy. (No research.) Career Mormons. The song Crazy Horse emulates a rock group thinking about being progressive.*

Doj Graham

They are singing Crazy Horses. It's like having Kancheli's Sixth[10] interrupted by the Lisa Marie Experience[11]. Some horror genres use this technique, the opening frame shocker to terrorize your emotions. All genres when I think a bit. What is the significance of milk in the film Komitas? Creativity cannot be researched, sometimes Komitas overfills me. It's not a film you can have Crazy Horses charging in through, or adverts…or eyeline distraction…neither smoke-filled rooms full (or empty) of mainstream critics whose understanding of contemplation, art tableaux, music are nil. Spilling milk in Armenia is an act of great folly and you shouldn't contemplate it.

2. Lost Highway

Especially the Lost. A new release unlike the other two films here. I saw this at the Duke of York's with Alanah[12], a Lynch completionist, a wonderfully comforting cinema with a very relaxing bar and comments book. There's a balcony, a good sound and they even let you take tea in. The sound in Pictureville[13] is better but the Duke has character and history and a real name like Essoldo[14]. History, like symbolism, cannot be researched. Only experience counts.

a. Content/Discontent.

The worst elements of modern day filmic dystopia prevail in Lost Highway. From the word go I couldn't get Kiss Me Deadly[15] out of my frame. The opening logos. The beach hut in flames. The tricky women. Never knowing where you are in relation to the plot. A film should have content… to digress, I love watching those independent films that Channel 4[16] sometimes do and various cinéthèques[17] still do.

---

*10. **Kancheli, Giya**. Living composer whose 3rd or maybe 6th Symphony carries a warning on the CD that there is extreme dynamic range. This is true but the music is deeply profound.*
*11. **The Lisa Marie Experience**. Appear on some Honking House or Banging Mansion compilation. Which even Trake rarely listens to.*
*12. **Alanah**. Alan J. Cowley - b. late sixties almost definitely. Probably the only living person who loves the ending of Thelma & Louise.*
*13. **Pictureville**. Bradford's fine cinema.*
*14. **Essoldo**. A chain of long gone cinemas. My memory is of the one in East Barnet.*
*15. **Kiss Me Deadly**. Classic film noir. Zonah could say "vra vra vroom" shortly after her second birthday.*
*16. **Channel 4**. TV staion that showed Sacrifice and Komitas.*
*17. **Cinéthèques**. General term to include all arthouse and hellhouse cinemas. By example, those at Cinematheque (Middle Street, Brighton), London Film Makers Co-op, Leicester Pheonix in early eighties and Plymouth Arts Centre, early eighties, probably now closed. Duke of Yorks (Brighton) on the other hand has given up its social and cultural wing and goes for audiences above 10, though in fairness it will produce films with live accompaniment and features oddities during the Brighton Festival, which redeems it.*

These films are often slow, weird, or technical exercises, or cut-ups, virtually anything can be expected. They rarely disappoint. In Lost Highway I could see no content. All I could see was an ego, or hear vapid music or assembled mythologies about cinema and not the film. Cinema as passive. Entertainment. Stars. When I wrote to the Duke of York's to find out what were the short films which came on before the Lost Highway feature I got no reply. These films were all mercurial and had me bemused. It's always nice, having shorts. Jack Nance[18] was again amongst the credits and everyone left the cinema long before the final credits. We came home both disillusioned.

b) The comfort of the Duke of York's. Arthouse cinema in Britain has long since been caught in a losing battle, forever compromising any radical screenings for ways to stay afloat. There I've said it.

3) Sacrifice

This is a film with no peers. I've seen it loads of times but mainly on video and never quite as cut up as mornings before work and as I'm an Otto this can be quite invigorating as well as surreal as you walk out into lonely Ashford Road [19], its cars all spread out over the tarmac like china breaking, the stars resonating in the heavens untouched (it would seem by anything remotely earthy). Otto is the postman in The Sacrifice (Sacrificio). And then afternoons when I'm not quite with it and evenings when I'm certainly not, and when fear, like the Osmonds, can eat your soul. The Little Man [20] is tying up Otto's bike as the pseudo-philosophy of the film goes downwind like the ever present rain. Elements, and indeed, spilt milk pervade this film and I've seen all Tarkovsky's films except The Steamroller and The Violin[21]. Will this ever be shown? How is it possible to view a work of art years removed from its original making? Why does less than popular music also follow this course of action? Can I be the only one to notice this? Fire eats up the log cabin and the flow of film, characters unfold. I think destroyed log cabins are the only connections in these two last films.

*18. **Jack Nance**. Actor. Probably living. Appeared in Eraserhead, a film which had a profound effect upon my relationship with Trake. That being that we split up for 5 months after seeing it.*
*19. **Ashford Road**. Brighton. Part of the 'Kent' streets. Dash in taxi parlance. Dover Ashford Sandgate and Hythe. No quasi-religiosity should be implied.*
*20. **Little Man**. Character in The Sacrifice giving credence to children in film which rarely happens in Hollywood. Why?*
*21. **Steamroller & The Violin**. Will this ever be shown?*

When I watch the Sacrifice I always want to understand more. About the things in life which interest me which I have no grasp upon but which have always intrigued me enough to find stained glass in a church, the uses and abuses of music, (to start with, film is only a beginning), for example. How better we can teach our children. Do they grow up on The Sound of Music [22] or The Spirit of the Beehive[23]?

a) This film has the weakest of Tarkovsky's endings yet it is a wonderful ending. One thing about the filmic experience is the closure. It's what you come away with and can euphorate you or deflate you completely. Luckily these three films are straightforward. Komitas leaves you in the balance, at the altar, but having set out its stall in the amazing intertitle sequence. It's a really potent closure and the mere word 'genocide' really strikes a tolling chord through me. Lost Highway leaves you in the vacuum you first entered, all those hours ago. Sacrifice points skywards and this is its point of weakness. Going up is flimsy. Ramming into a tree as in Ivan's Childhood [24] is nerve-wracking and hurts (in your heart). The end of Stalker[24] sees the power in the metaphysical (never far away in A.T.). That all-encompassing forest in Mirror [24] actually breathes at the end. This Sacrifice ending is too tame and the sentimental (presumption of death) captions are a Hollywoodian cringe. However it is allowable. Seven amazing films is enough for anyone.

4. When a camera looks for footholds you know you are in a land of detour. From thinking, mainly. From connecting with those things which make us human even if this entails some connection with the greatest of all unexplained mysteries the time honoured indulging of religion. Two of these films openly and broadly sweep religion, the very thing I'm most sceptical of. The one that doesn't is a total detour, of fantasy and irrelevance. To slow down enough to think is something we all rarely do. Thinking in segments of fractured viewing of contemplative films is surely a prescription for therapy. My wife is a pharmaceutical chemist. Neither of us apologize.

---

22. ***The Sound of Music***. *Politically astute film of precise Austrian culture.*
23. ***The Spirit of the Beehive***. *Classic. Zonah readily identifies with Anna. (Worryingly.)*
24. ***Ivan's Childhood***. ***Stalker***. ***Mirror***. *The other three are Andrei Rublev, in which everything - music, film, art - are revelatory, Solaris and Nostalgia, of which Zonah has only seen the dream sequences in Ivan, the fence breaking to the children drinking milk in Mirror.*

Finally I've seen all David Lynch's films mainly with Trake and Alanah, though he's never seen The Grandmother or Alphabet. But I never watched Twin Peaks. Don Askarjan who directed Komitas I know nothing of.

The Black Room

ACT ONE

(The entire action takes place in a bare-bricked room, without a door. The room has no light-source or window, and is - in reality - completely darkened. Hence, for theatrical purposes, the lighting is very low. RON, the sole inhabitant of the room, can only be fully seen occasionally, and is mostly just a voice-in-the-darkness". RON's face is dirty as a long-term beggar's. He resembles Ben Gunne, with long wild hair, a tatty T-shirt and 1970's flared 'loons'.)

RON RAWLINGS:

My name is… My name ….. My name is… …..Ron!
It Was 1974. I was 18. Frank was two years older. My brother, Frank, and me both went to Crete on holiday that summer. Both of us had flared loons and sandals, and hair that made us look like King Charles spaniels.
Originally the plan was to sleep on the beach like free spirits. But we got a package tour instead, and due to a booking error ended up in a family room, with three beds and a cot.
The very first night we saw these two girls in a bar. They noticed us too.
And looked up… and immediately went back to their conversation, in the way that girls do. Thinking they might be Germans, Frank spoke in the slowed-down-English that we think foreigners will understand.
"May… We join.. You?"
(ENGLISH GIRL) "Ar'you Scandinavians?!"
"No, from Croydon" I said.
"We're from Bedford. I'm Rowena and this is my best friend - Carol".
Bang! The first time I heard Carol's name. And ever since. Everytime. I hear it. Say it. Think it: A gun goes off in my head. Carol: Bang!
Carol - Bang - was a bit unfortunate to look at in the first instance, on account of the nervous tick. Her nose twitched virtually continually for about fifteen minutes. Poor girl, she seemed oblivious of it. But after we'd been chatting for a bit she seemed to relax and it stopped. Rowena was nervous too - and kept nibbling on the beer mat. The rest of the evening was complete chaos. Because both Frank and me were going for Carol. Every little moment was a triumph or a disaster.
"Do you want a drink Carol ?"
(CAROL) "Yes please".

Bang: Yes!

"Carol? Do you want another drink?"

(CAROL) "No thanks, but Rowena will have one".

The very opposite of Bang.

Carol was thinking of doing physics at university. I said: "Physics, urgh! Science is shit. We had a physics teacher at school, who ran the Christian Union, who threw us out of the classroom at lunchtime for telling a dirty joke. And do you know what the joke was?… What do you call a Spanish woman with one tooth? …One-Eater".

(PHYSICS TEACHER) "Get out of here with that filthy, dis-gusting talk !"

"Well, that's got fuck all to do with physics, has it ?" said Carol. "That bloke was just a sexually repressed Christian who secretly wanted oral sex from a Mexican woman".

Carol had said "oral-sex": Bang! Carol really lit up when she talked about atoms, electrons, neutrons and protons. And when she said "Quark", I wanted to kiss her. By midnight we were all on the beach and drunk. We'd just built a twenty foot wide sand sculpture: a smiley face in relief. The idea being that if flying saucers were passing overhead that's where they would decide to land. And Frank was crawling in and out of the water. Re-enacting a documentary he'd seen… about how giant turtles laid their eggs in the sand. And he was making Carol laugh. By dawn we were lying there waiting for the sun to come up, and Carol was trying to explain Einstein's Theory of General Relativity. That was the moment I knew I loved her. It was the sexiest thing I'd ever heard:

"Einstein's theory of general relativity proves that gravity is not a force, as Newton believed, but the curvature of four dimensional space-time…" Frank was unashamedly looking at Carol's breasts by this time. But I remembered my Grandfather saying to me when I was fourteen: "Stolen glances of a woman's body can kill her, Ron…. That's how Marilyn Monroe died. After a Marilyn Monroe film, the movie audiences came away with such a vivid picture of Marilyn, in their minds' eyes, that little by little, all of herself was removed, bit by bit, and she became a husk and died. Marilyn Monroe was killed by being looked at too much, Ron. And, if that's true, they'd have to hang millions of us for the crime of it!"

I didn't want to kill Carol. I loved her. So I just looked at her eyes. And her face. And her breasts.

On our last night I thought I knew Carol well enough to ask about the twitching.

"Do you know your nose…? It twitches. Is it a nervous thing or what ?"

(CAROL) "No. Morse Code."

"Hm ?"

(CAROL) "Dots and dashes".

"Huh ?"

(CAROL) "Well, If I want to tell Rowena something…"
"Oh, I see! So, when me and Frank first came over.…?"
(CAROL) "I told Rowena I fancied you…(TWITCHES NOSE) Then I asked her if she fancied Frank? (TWITCHES NOSE) If she did, she had to signal ……. (TWITCHES NOSE) by biting the beer mat".
I asked Carol to say "Quark". And kissed her. We met up with Frank and Rowena, a bit red faced. Frank looked daggers at me. Carol's nose started twitching. Rowena laughed. I laughed. And Frank said: "What the fuck are you lot laughing at ?!" And stormed off. That night, back in the family room, Frank was complaining about having lost his Led Zeppelin tape. I said:
"Frank. There's only one Carol!"
(FRANK) "Yeah, I know. And it looks like I'm going to have to kill you to get her, doesn't it, Ron?!!
Then we had a stupid wrestling fight on the bed, like we used to do in the old days, and Frank admitted that he'd done more than a bit of snogging with Rowena.

*

I was thinking about Carol all the time when we'd come back from Crete. As far as I was concerned, from what Carol had told me about physics, there was a steady stream of love-atoms trekking valiantly across the space between us, between Croydon and Bedford. Maybe love founders when the little love-atoms can't be bothered to go around all the electricity pylons and across all the motorways on the way to reaching their destinations. I was on the phone all the time.
"Have they arrived? The love atoms? I sent another big party out this morning?"
(CAROL) "Ron, atoms do not have little legs."
"Mine do".
Our longest call was two and a half days. By the end, we were just sitting there, listening to the silence.
"Well, it's dawn here, Carol".
(CAROL) "It's still dark here, Ron".
"There's definitely a sliver of orange here, Carol. Yep. It's dawn in Croydon
(CAROL) "Ron?"
"What ?"
(CAROL) "It's coming up here now."
We started living together, in Croydon, just before Christmas 1975. We thought the best way of celebrating Christmas was the traditional pagan way - of fasting for two days, then drinking a bottle of whiskey through the Queen's Speech. Both me and Frank had inherited a little money from our parents. I bought a house. Frank was planning to invest his. He wanted to start a business buying up farmhouses in France and doing them up. Me and Carol set up home. The first thing we bought was a kitchen table; which Carol insisted was, on an atomic level, an integral part

of the whole universe. Technically speaking, the table was infinitely big.
"Yes, but we still got it through the door though, didn't we?"
Carol didn't go to university. She went into social work. Until one day a skinhead girl attacked her with a table tennis bat, and Carol decided she wanted to teach primary school kids.
(CAROL) "Atoms, kids: they're both small and fascinating, Ron."
I was planning to do a course in Town Planning, but was worried about having to get my hair cut, to get a proper job.
(CAROL) "Don't let the squares do all the important jobs, Ron".
"Yeah, but they're not going to let me build cities like these, are they?" I said, holding up some sketches I'd done… of futuristic cities, inspired by pictures of copulating insects. Then she told me. She was pregnant.
It was 1975, I was nineteen, and I was striding along in my new black crushed velvet loons, flapping in the breeze. Jimi Hendrix t-shirt. Feeling like life was a drug and that this was how you were meant to feel. My girlfriend Carol - Bang - had just told me she was pregnant. And I was going down the shops and planning on making some ratatouille. I was coming back from Sainsburys. It was the second week of June, the Thursday, if anyone remembers it. I took the short cut down the alleyway, down the side of Sainsburys, which led to the back, where the loading bays were. And I heard the sound of a baby crying. There was nobody around. There was a transit van, with the back doors wide open, and there on the floor inside, was a tape-recorder… with the sound of a baby crying, coming out of it…. A bag went over my head. Then there was this sound, like somebody hitting the top of a bowler hat with their knuckles. A hollow thud. Thuck! I quickly realised that someone had hit me on the head…. I saw a tree with birds sitting on all the branches suddenly take flight all at once.
I've often wondered about this, and can only think that I'd been hit on the exact part of the head where you store the memories of birds taking flight from trees. Everything went black. I woke up. Everything was black. I took the bag off my head. Everything was still black. I opened my eyes. Still black. I must have tried to open my eyes a hundred times. Until I got a headache. Because they were open. I was in a room. There was no light. Just blackness. And that was where I spent the next 15 years. No company, no sex. Just my own thoughts for 15 years !!! Still, you've got to try and keep cheerful, haven't you ? Try and keep your sense of humour?

ACT TWO

I was lying there with a lump on my head, feeling dead. I got up tentatively, like a blind man, unable to see my hand in front of my face. I found the walls. Four of them. But no door. Not a chink of light. Not a draft. No keyhole. I frisked all the walls and didn't find a light switch. The utter darkness made my eyes panic. I totally lost all sense of up and down. The thought crossed my mind that my feet were on the ceiling… and I fell over. I screamed. Hammered. Got tired. And fell asleep. Thinking of Carol.

*

Carol must have been going spare. The police station. The sleepless nights. The doubts. No body found. In a ditch? Or down a drain? No ransom notes! Detectives inferring that she might not know me well enough to categorically say that I hadn't disappeared off somewhere, to start a new life, somewhere else, without telling her.
(DETECTIVE) "I'm sorry Carol, as a detective I have to conclude that Ron is probably dead. It makes me sick this kind of thing. Sick! I really am sorry your boyfriend is dead, Carol. By the way, what are you doing Saturday night ?" But Carol had Frank, and Rowena. She had Frank and Rowena! Frank and Rowena would look after her.
"But Frank fancied Carol" said the-Cleverer-Than-You-Are voice in my head. The next morning - which could have been the middle of the afternoon for all I knew - I woke up, and the-Cleverer-Than-You-Are voice in my head, said:
"Still Here Then?"

In sheer desperation I got up and ran. One step, two steps - Bang. I hit the wall sooner than I expected. I couldn't even see my hand in front of my face. Or the sticky warm stuff on my fingers. I gave the room another frisking in case I'd missed the light switch or overlooked a concealed window. Or French windows, leading onto a balcony overlooking the Mediterranean! Then I found it! In the corner. It was an animal. I stood there. Terrified. Worrying about what was going to happen when the animal woke up…………!! It was a mattress. How could I have missed a mattress in a ten foot square room ?!!
The room was featureless. Smooth concrete walls and floor. The only distinguishing feature was a foot tall door at the bottom of one wall. I consoled myself that I would have found it sooner if I'd been a foot tall! Inside the little door was a round-sided-plastic-thing. Which turned out to be a plastic bucket. Which turned out to be full of things. Which turned out to be bread and cheese and fruit. Even a can of fizzy drink. Lemon flavour. And there were a couple of shiny-spongy things, that I couldn't identify, that I didn't eat, until I got desperate. They were aubergines.

I finished the whole bucket full. Comfort-eating I suppose you'd call it. Then I shouted obscenities for a long while, and got a stitch. There was the sound like a rifle bolt being drawn back, or the clunk of a chocolate vending machine drawer being pulled out. The hole had closed. Then another sound. A second bucket! Of water with a towel. Then a third bucket. Empty. For piss and shit. Over the years I prayed for one thing. That they kept those buckets separate.

The prospects of escaping were grim. My pockets were empty. All I had in the way of a tool was the zip on my crushed velvet loons. And they don't use the best quality zips in the first place. And as a digging implement it was rubbish. I wasn't going to dig my way out with a zip, was I?

What I craved for, really craved for, more than human contact, beer, sex, anything, was a swiss army penknife. It became an obsession. Why aren't we born with one? Why don't we have a small specially designed flap of skin on our leg, like a pocket in a pair of dungarees. With a Swiss Army Penknife in it? For that matter, why haven't we got public callboxes in our chest cavities? So that we can call-up for help, wherever we are? Why can't we take out the bones in our legs and slot two of them together to make a pick-axe, so that we can dig our way out of any situation? God! Why are human beings so defenceless?

"Because: some thug would come along and use *their* Swiss Army Penknife to vandalise your phone. Then lock you up, then take away your pick-axe legs. And then you'd be in the same situation you are in now, but not able to walk…. !" said the-Cleverer-Than-You-Are-Voice-In-My-Head.

I tried to coax a little conversation out of whoever it was:

"Why is this happening? Who are you? A nun? Emptying my shit and piss bucket, then putting aubergines in the same bucket, and saying: I'm just off to feed the Anti-Christ!"

"What have I done? Who are you? Do you know why you're doing this? Tell me *why* you are doing this? If you tell me… maybe I believe in the same thing… the same cause… then you could let me out. We could go and have a beer together! Then we could *both* go around locking people up, for whatever reason it is?! Why are you doing this?! Why me? Why the darkness? This is Ron Rawlings!! Who do you think I am?!' It was so dark that I quickly began to forget who I was. I was born 1955…

Me, and my brother Frank, had an inauspicious start in life. We grew up near Gatwick Airport in Crawley. One day, in 1960, our Mum was out in the garden. She'd just put out the sun lounger, and put on the suntan lotion, when an aeroplane took off. As its undercarriage closed, one wheel hadn't retracted, and it came off… Our Mum had just that second laid down and closed her eyes when the wheel came bouncing over the hedge and - Smack!

Plate 9   Greg Daville. House of the Spirits
Collage (24 x 17 in.)

Plate 10   Lynne Gibson. The Quester
Etching/Aquatint/Collagraph (13 x 8 in.)
After the poem *In Defence of the Raven* by Peter Abbs

Plate 11   Lynne Gibson. The Starwort Shirt
Etching/Aquatint/Collagraph (12 x 6 in.)
Inspiration for *Fallen Man with One Wing* by Peter Abbs

Plate 12   Lynne Gibson. Icarus at the Big Top
Etching/Aquatint/Collagraph (19 x 13 in.)
After the poem *Wittgenstein's Furniture* by Peter Abbs

Plate 13   Drew Hewitt. Cirkus Family
Acrylic/Pastel on paper (41 x 29in.)

Plate 14 Drew Hewitt. This Sporting Life
Acrylic/Pastel on paper (41 x 41in.)

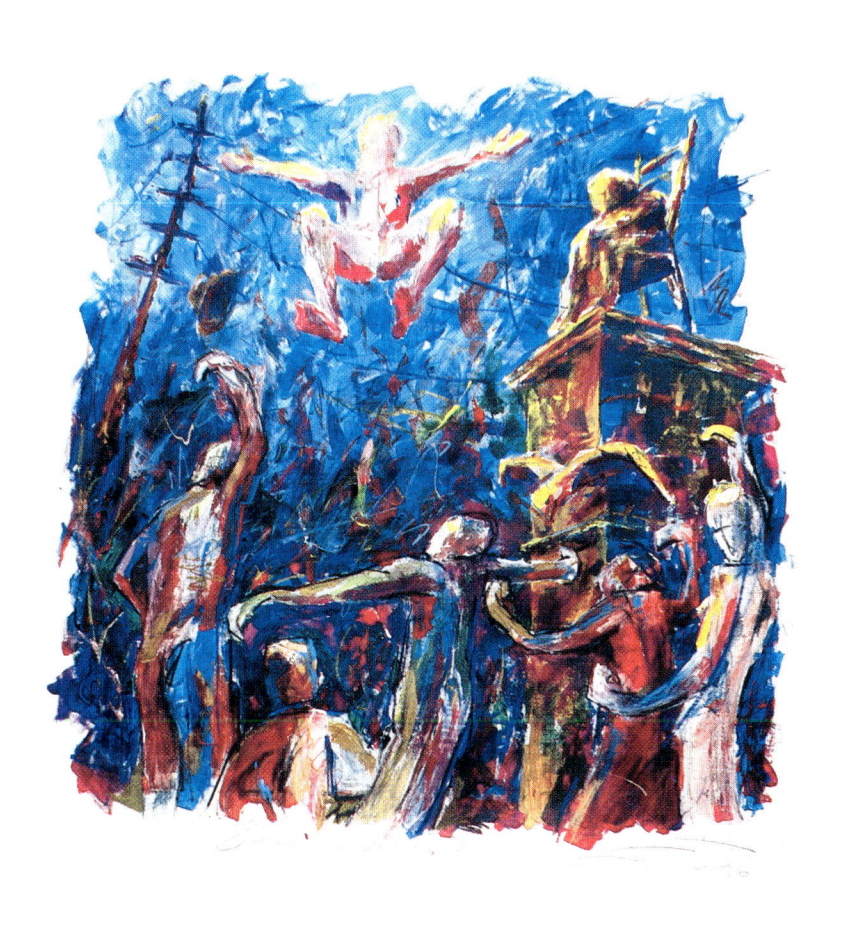

Plate 15 Drew Hewitt. The Levitator
Acrylic/Pastel on paper (32 x 31in.)
In the collection of Matthew & Tina Longman

Plate 16 Greg Daville. Proposed Monument to Love
Collage (24 x 17 in.)

The wheel continued, bouncing-bomb fashion, smashed through the upstairs bathroom window and went down the stairs, just as Dad opened the front door, coming home from work ! At the inquest, they reckoned Dad must have seen it coming and frozen with terror. His neck muscles were so tense that it snapped off his head like a twig. Me and Frank came home from school and saw the people across the road looking at their bashed in garage doors and we laughed. Because our garage was opposite theirs and when they were out we used their garage for a goal. Which they didn't like. At first Frank and me thought Dad was just having a laugh, like the year before in Jersey on holiday, when he buried himself up to the neck in the sand. But your Dad's head shouldn't be sat in the flower beds. And his body shouldn't be leant against the door post like a shop dummy. He was still awake, and looked up at us and said:

(DAD) "I think the compost I put on the roses yesterday is just about sealing up my neckhole and keeping the blood in my brain, boys".

Dad knew all about medical things and gardening. Me and Frank looked at each other, and vaguely tried to remember the word for 'orphan'.

(DAD) "Promise me you'll look after each other. And give all my love to your Mum". We both knelt down and kissed him goodbye. Then we found Mum in the back garden. Despite her being spread out a bit she looked very peaceful. Her head was still intact as well and had ended up balanced on the cloches where she grew her tomatoes. It must have been squeezed off by the impact, like the top off toothpaste.

(MUM) "And where do you think you've been ? You should have been home an hour ago !"

We kissed Mum And told her that Dad said he loved her. Frank said it would have been quite nice if we'd all have been hit by that aeroplane wheel and died as a family. Mum was so accepting and beautiful about it. And before she died she pulled a stupid face and made us both laugh.

After the funeral we went to see *Snow White and the Seven Dwarfs*. When I was a kid, whenever there was a big family funeral, after the service we'd all go to the pictures together. Years later when my grandmother died there was a really big crowd; people came from as far away as Ireland, and we all went to see *Bambi*. A lot of the grown ups snook off to the pub. But there were a lot of kids, and I think someone wanted to keep our young minds off the subject of death, see it as more of a celebration, more of an outing. People dying was always associated with films. Auntie Freda was *Chitty Chitty Bang Bang*. Uncle Leonard was *2000 Years BC*. And Cousin Robert was… *Straw Dogs*, I think it was.

After that, me and Frank went to live with our Grandfather. Our grandfather let us call him Tom. Tom was a huge man, tall and wide. He had to stoop to get through the doors. And when he sat down in the armchair he looked like a cow wearing

Tony Haase

clothes. Tom was very religious. But after he'd had a few pints he would get maudlin and menacing:
(GRANDFATHER) "Life is full of choices. Moral choices, like forks in the road. If you do a good thing, Ron, you go along the path of righteousness, but if you do a bad thing, Frank, you go down the path to damnation!"
I said:
"But what if you did a good thing one day, then a bad thing the next day, Tom, are there suddenly two of you, going off down separate paths, Tom?"
"Don't be so bloody stupid, Ron" said Frank.
But the idea got to me. I had an identical double, someone who thought they were me, walking down the road to damnation. I guess I just had an overly excitable imagination… which is just the sort of character trait you want, isn't it, when you're locked in a Black Room?

I was six. It was 1961. And I lived in terror. I had an understandable fear of things falling from the skies. Me and Frank used to try and scare each other. It was a kind of hobby. We'd lie in bed looking at the ceiling.
"Frank, if there were two swimming pools. And you had to jump into one of them. And one was full of shit, the other full of sick: which one would you jump in?"
"The sick one", said Frank, without hesitating.
(FRANK) "Ron, do you know what happens in the night Ron, when you're asleep? Grandad and Grandma turn into giant insects. They do it whenever you're not around. I've seen them. And they creep into your bedroom, Ron, with their horrible pincers twitching, and stand over you, dribbling. Because if Grandad loses his job again… if there was no money… and no food in the cupboard… When Sunday comes and there was no dinner… They've decided, because you're the youngest, Ron… to eat you! And you'll go screaming into the oven ! Within a week, in a hotpot, with salads, and Grandad's sandwiches… You'll be all gone, Ron. And I'll go to school and say: "I don't know where Ron is, Miss, he just ran off somewhere."
"I don't know where Ron is, Miss, he just ran off somewhere… I don't know where Ron is, Miss, he just ran off somewhere."

I thought my Grandfather, Tom, was the most educated man in the world. Despite the fact that he lived in a basement flat in Croydon and was a cabinet maker, he loved opera. He'd even written an opera. Despite having had no musical training or any musical knowledge whatsoever. As a kid I always remember Tom coming home smelling of wood glue. He'd put on a record on his old gramophone and stand looking at his beetroot plants in the garden. After a while he'd say:
(GRANDFATHER) "Listen to that bloody woman sing, Ron. That's a big voice.

That voice is making men's knackers vibrate as far away as France. If you're down in the dumps, Ron, *sing!*"

It was a month before before me and Frank went to Crete. I was still living at home. Over tea, Uncle Tom produced a great pile of manuscript paper and dumped it on my lap. It was his opera.
It was written on musical manuscript paper, but didn't look like a musical score. It was just a bunch of descriptions. Like… 'Overture: A little jaunty hummy bit, with drums way off, like drunks almost too far away to be heard. But definitely coming towards you. Then all of a sudden there's the whole caboodle: cellos, violins, drums, going: Ka-kaa-dreee…. ohhhh!'
"Ka-kaa-dreee-ohhhh ?" I said.
"Ka-Kaa-Dreee…..Ohhhh !" sang Tom.
(GRANDFATHER) "I don't know the notes. It obviously needs working out with the orchestra. But I've described the effect I want. Should be enough for a decent singer to get their teeth into, don't you think, Ron ?

The week before me and Frank went to Crete, my grandmother died. The whole Irish branch of the family came over. Tom, my grandfather, was taken pretty bad by it. Me and Frank went to the funeral parlour with him We stood there looking at our grandmother lying in the coffin.
(GRANDFATHER) "She looks like she might open her eyes, doesn't she ?" said Tom.
(GRANDFATHER) "Oi, wake up, love!"
Tom started slapping her around the face. The undertakers threatened to phone the police. But Tom was insistent.
(GRANDFATHER) "Listen mate, I'm her husband, I'm just checking she isn't fooling about, alright? Now… Wake up, love! Wake up ! Wake up !"
After the funeral we all walked down the road.
(GRANDFATHER) "I never laid a finger on your grandmother - when she was alive", said Tom. "And there's those paid sympathisers accusing me of wife beating. I'm not having her going in the ground still alive. It's an infuriating thing. The infuriating reluctance of dead people to walk around and talk. Forty for *Bambi* please".

Tom grabbed me by the hand, and said, holding it, as if he was passing on his whole life: "If you're down in the dumps Ron, *sing!*"
That's who I am !!!

But there was never a response. Nothing. Ever.

The Cleverer-Than-You-Are voice in my head finally lost his bottle.
"This is the best place in the world. You hear that, you motherfuckers! I'm really enjoying this in here! You're missing out on something out there. This is where the party is. You fucking bastards! I can't it stand any more...!!!"
He broke down totally. That voice, he really wept. I thought I was going down and never coming up. I lay down on the floor, wretched, abject, pitiful.
And very quietly the voice in my head, as if on his deathbed, said:
"We'll fool these fuckers, whoever they are"
"You mean you were faking that ?"
"Keep your voice down, Ron. Never let them know what you're feeling. We're going to get through this, you and me. We're going to survive. We're going to live."

Then the hallucinations began. A pit of fear opened up beneath, as big as the floor and as deep as time. The whole floor gave way. Like you're sitting there and the whole floor is going down a lift shaft.... Ahhhh! A tower of rooms like a block of flats going back in time. Bang - down through to trapdoor to the floor below. Bang - the room below. Bang - the room below that.
Trapdoors banging open under your feet. You falling down. Down. Bang. Down. Bang. Into the room where the cavemen mindlessly thwack-in skulls. Bang. Bang. Bang. Blood and matted hair. Bang. The room below. The cavemen hiding behind the tree and the man walking innocently along. Bang the room below. No cavemen behind the tree. No man. Bang. The room below. No tree. Nothing. Splosh. Bang. Bottom. And the floor is treacle and you are sinking into an infinitely deep devil's bumhole of a thing.

"If you're down in the dumps Ron, *sing*." It started in a small way. A little humming... Kaa-kaa-dree-ohhh...
Kaa-kaa-dree-ohhh...
Kaa-kaa-dree-ohhh...
Produced a few little twigs, in my mind, which I collected up: Kaa-kaa-dreeohhh... An imaginary cigarette lighter with a flip top. Kaa-kaa-dree-ohhh. Little flames flickering in the darkness. Kaa-kaa-dree-ohhh ! I got better at it. Kaa-kaa-dree-ohhh!!! Everything I wanted. I sang it. Kaa-kaa-dree-ohhh!!!!! An imaginary Carol walked in! Kaa-kaa-dree-ohhh !!!!!!
(The only worry I had with my imaginary Carol was the mortifying thought: I couldn't remember what colour her eyes were. Grey, I thought). Kaa-kaa-dree-ohhh !!!!!!!! And so they were. Kaa-kaa-dree-ohhh!!!!!!!!!!!!!!!!
"Ron. I'm pregnant" said Carol.

"Sit down, rest. I'll cook some ratatouille for tea."
Kaa-kaa-dree-ohhh…
And I went down the shops feeling life was a drug and this was how you were meant to feel. I went down the side of Sainsburys. And I heard a baby crying. There was a transit van with the back doors wide open, and there inside on the floor was a tape-recorder, with the sound of a baby crying coming out of it. I turned around and there was Frank, with a baseball bat and a sack.
"Hello Ron, I thought it was you" said Frank.

Carol had the baby. We called him Bob. I was heavily involved in town planning, and Croydon town centre had been remodelled on the theme of giant insects copulating. Not everybody liked it. I was concerned about the dangers of cars on children, so I worked in the traffic department. Kaa-kaa-dree-oohh!
I put forward my ideas at a town council meeting: "Maybe one solution is: we find out the numbers of people killed each year by cars and then randomly select the same number of drivers - and put them to death publicly. Either that, or we persuade the car manufacturers to redesign the body work of all cars to look like turds. To make the self image of being a driver less compelling is the idea, the psychology being that people wouldn't want to sit at the wheel of something that looked like a piece of shit."

And so, it was a world where children were indestructible. A world where children could even put their necks on railway lines and get run over, and not even have a scratch on them. I was toddling down the road. Bob had just learnt to walk. An old lady jumped out of a block of flats from a 15th floor window. Splat! She got up, dusted herself down:
(OLD LADY) "It's quicker than getting the lift. Isn't he a nice little boy? What's his name?"
"Bob."
Our son, Bob, was five and he was a beautiful distraction. One day he came in from the garden and said: "Hello Daddy". He was all covered in leaves and oil. (TO BOB) "Have you been putting your neck on the line again Bob?"
(BOB) "Yes Daddy".

That night, me and Carol leant against the door post watching Bob's little breathing. He was lying in bed like he'd just been shot in a war film. I had to ask Carol. I had to be sure.
"Carol, if ever I went missing, and you didn't know whether I was dead or had just run off, how long would you wait before you gave up on me, Carol?"
(CAROL) "Forever Ron. Forever."

Life was perfect. Everything was perfect. But I still had the nagging doubt. I went to the police station. I told them I wanted to report a missing person.

(POLICEMAN) "So, sir, this Ron Rawlings who went missing. You believe he is locked up somewhere against his will?"
"Yes, definitely against his will."
(POLICEMAN) "I see sir. And your name is?"
"Ron Rawlings".
(POLICEMAN) "Would I be right in thinking that you are the same person that you are reporting missing, sir?"
"Yes. I've been kidnapped and locked in a black room, but I don't know where".
The police officer was remarkably understanding.
(POLICEMAN) "Would this be a world parallel to this one, sir ? Like this one in every respect, even with my own double living there?"
"Yes, officer. Yes, that's it!"
(POLICEMAN) "Then all I can suggest, sir, is that you go to the police station in that world, sir, and speak to my double there about it."
"The thing is, officer, even if I could get through to that parallel world and went to a police station there. Even if I got through, they'd say the same thing, wouldn't they? If you're missing, how come you're here, sir. Either way I look stupid!"
(POLICEMAN) "That is the nature of your dilemma, sir. I would love to be able to help you sir, but I'm afraid my jurisdiction stops short of other worlds."
It was the last thing I wanted - to go mad. Especially with a budding career in town planning ahead of me. When I got home, Rowena and Frank were there. I was a bit pissed and it was getting late, but I had to get it off my chest:
"Do you know what happened years ago? I was coming back from Sainsbury's through the short cut when I heard this baby crying. Everything went black. I woke up. Everything was still black. I took the bag off my head. Everything was still black. I opened my eyes, again and again, until I got a headache, because they were open. And that's where I've been, locked up in a black room." Everybody was staring at me.
"What are you saying, love?" said Carol
"About five years ago, before Bob was born, Carol, I went to the shops and I didn't come back. I know it sounds crazy. It was that day I met you, Frank, when you had the baseball bat and the sack".
(FRANK) "Ron, please, what are you trying to say? Why would I want to kidnap my own brother?"
"Well, with me out of the way, say for ten years, Carol would be all alone and you could…"

Tony Haase

(FRANK) "Oh that's nice, Ron. That's lovely…"
"Then what were you doing by that transit van…. with the baseball bat and the sack, Frank?!'
Frank and I stood looking at each other like boxers. As Frank spoke I could smell his breath going up my nose:
(FRANK) "You think I kidnapped you, Ron, and have got you locked up in a parallel world, is that it?!"
"Yes. I do. Answer me honestly, Frank".
(FRANK)…. "No, Ron."

The infuriating ability of people to not tell the truth on purpose! I picked up Frank by the feet and swung him around smashing all the furniture in the room. Carol and Rowena looked on aghast from the kitchen doorway as I smashed down the walls of the house, using Frank as a club. After I'd knocked down the whole house, I started on the town - and left Croydon in rubble. After that… I went on a world wide rampage that left the entire planet in ruins, and everybody in it dead! Frank was just a bit of bone in my hand. A leg bone covered in blood and a bit of matted hair. Carol and Rowena came running down the road:
(CAROL & ROWENA) "Ron, Please, Stop!"
I wept. And thrashed. And screamed:
"All you oppressors and jailers will continue forever oppressing and jailing till a million years of regret will snap you like twigs. You cannot escape. I can escape. You lock me up. But I can be free. But you never can be. In all the black places in all the world the bent and broken and suffering sit in solitude and speak through the darkness to each other. We can bear everthing you throw at us. We will absorb every punishment. We can escape. But you cannot get away with anything. The sky is black with your injustices come back to haunt you…

Tony Haase

ACT THREE

"Ron!" said the Cleverer-Than-You-Are voice in my head.
"What?!"
"Frisk the room".
"Again?!!"
"Ron, frisk the room!!'."
And there in the lining of my Afghan coat was a lump. My front door key had fallen through into the lining of my coat. And I started scratching away at the mortar between the bricks. A little, often, mounts up to a lot, and finally the brick moved….

The oblong shaped hole with the light shining in, singing in. I pulled the bricks loose and clambered through the hole. I crawled up some stairs. And emerged in a house, with no carpets, bare boards, a few pieces of furniture, mice. Mice and dust. Wasn't dust good to look at?! Grimey windows that you couldn't see out of. My hands groped towards the door handle, eyes screwed tight, the front door creaked open and…. there was the sky! The house was on a tree-lined road. Trees disappearing off in both directions to the horizon. Perspective! When you turned around: there it was. The world. No matter how you try and trick it, and look around quickly: it was there. I stood there in the middle of the road. My crushed velvet loons flapping in the breeze. My hair and beard down to my waist. Looking like Ben Gunne. The whole scene was astonishing. Sky, clouds, trees, the earth. It all fitted together, like a symphony…. or a fish. And I set off like that road was a road to heaven. Walking ten feet at a time. A car went past with French number plates. Five more went past with French number plates. I decided it was more than a coincidence, and said to myself:

"I must be in France !"
I thought, a little egocentrically, that everybody in the world had just heard what I'd said. Then I said, measuring my words:
"This is Ron Rawlings speaking to the whole world, I have been away but now I am back. I will be seeing all of you very shortly."
There couldn't have been anybody for miles around but I felt like some formal announcement had to be made. Off I trudged, listening to the music pouring out of everything I saw. I arrived in Dieppe walking and singing all the way. Two days and nights non-stop. It was early morning and there was a smell of coffee and sweet pastry in the air when I saw the sea, green and grey, with England cleverly concealed over the horizon.

Croydon! The streets were full of people wearing tracksuits. Was the Olympics being held in Croydon? And the building society had women behind the counter

dressed like redcoats. After some explaining the manager allowed me to sign my name, and said:
(MANAGER) "You're the kind of saver we like Mr. Rawlings".
Suddenly I had £600 in my account, where previously I had only £3.50. I wandered into the sports shop…
"Excuse me, I want to get my son a present. He's…. fifteen now."
(SHOP ASSISTANT) "How about an American football, or a baseball bat, sir?"
"Er, I'll take the bat. Excuse me, I've been away. Have the Americans taken over completely?"
I strolled towards Kendal Street. Sunny streets. One house had been sort of turned into a sort of castle. I smiled at everyone. I turned into my road. My road. As far as my girlfriend was concerned - 15 years ago, the day after she told me she was pregnant - I went to the shops and didn't come back. It doesn't exactly put you in a good light, does it?

Was she living with someone else by now? Of course she was. Was she even living there anymore? Probably not. I went to the park. One hour I decided I would wait, and then I'd go and find out. What was one hour in the sunshine compared to fifteen years in the dark? I had the sort of expression that a statue wears in a park. Not a lack of enjoyment, more of the expression that indicated that the statue would still have to be there when everybody else went home. As a kid I felt sorry for statues in parks, having to keep the same expression on their faces all the time, and having to keep their jackets on in really hot weather. The hour had passed. And the statue left the park.
I walked down my street and arrived at the front door. The sliver of front door key… fitted! The hallway appeared like a Dutch interior. The door to the living room swung open, like a door to the living-room. The living-room and the back room had been knocked through. At the far end, with a table full of papers in front of him, sat Frank.
Without turning round, he said:
"Carol?"

It's strange how things work out. If only I hadn't had a baseball bat in my hand. The bat was in my hands. And a blackness filled my blood. I walked towards him slowly raising the bat. A thwack came into my mind that was 15 years long. The baseball bat came down on Frank's unsuspecting head. His head hit the table.
"Mum?!"
A teenage girl stood in kitchen doorway holding a cup of tea.
(CAROL) "What was that, love?" A woman appeared at the girl's shoulder. It was Carol. Bang! Her eyes were grey. Bang!

Tony Haase

Mum? What was that, love? Daughter? Me?

"Ron?" said Carol.

"Dad!?" said The Girl.

"Daughter? I've got a daughter?"

"Ron, this is… Penny" said Carol. The blood from Frank's head flowed to the edges of the table and dripped to the floor making a perfect circle of blood on the carpet.

"Penny? Where's Bob?!"

After Frank's funeral we all went to see *Back To The Future*. Carol and Penny came to visit me in prison. Through the glass, Carol's nose twitched:

"I… Love… You… Ron."

Despite what Frank had done, and despite the fact he was dead, I badly wanted him to visit me. And when it was dark he did come.

(FRANK) "You'll be out in a few years Ron, but me…"

"Frank, one thing. The buckets. Did you ever mix up the buckets, on purpose, even for a laugh?"

"No…" said Frank, getting up to go.

(FRANK) "Before I go for good, Ron, I want to know. How did you do it, Ron?"

"Door key. Front door key, in the lining of my Afghan coat, Frank."

We hugged and Frank walked off into the darkness, muttering: "Key in the lining of his coat. Key in the lining of his coat. Door key in the lining of his coat…"

"But, Ron" said the Cleverer-Than-You-Are voice in my head…

"You *weren't* wearing a coat."

FADE TO BLACK

The Seabirds' Chorus

A night of rain, and then
a day of rain, hanging in rails
over the blackened hills;

clouds like anvils,
black at the centre, purple-edged.
The downpour drills

the sodden upland and spills
into the bowl of the valley.
A sudden rush of rainfall swills

the foreshore and fills
the hoop of the sky so that it melds
with the sea. It cancels

a mile of cliffs; it blots out sails;
it batters thresholds;
it clambers over sills;

it takes the high ground in squalls;
it swamps the furnaces
of landmills and seamills.

If this is the end of the world,
it will rain until
the world is purged, and still

rain so that nothing remains
but the nub of field and fell
and water does whatever it will

Already it beats underground.
Already it seems to shrill
in the yardpump and the well.

The world will be waterfalls
till Doomsday breaks. Listen -
the sound of the rain is endless bells.

David Harsent

The Scientist's Song

There's a fury sleeping in rock;
we dug a conduit for that.

There's a doctrine in ebb and flow;
we found a method for that.

There's a swiftness in grasslands and uplands;
we constructed a harness for that.

There's a richness in the tree-canopy;
we put down railways and airstrips.

There's a fragrance in deltas;
we took it to a distillery.

There's opulence in a dustmote,
in a dot of pollen, in a spore of moss;
we harvested that,
we built a silo for that.

The buttercup's blueprint,
the wing's aftermath,
the rainstorm's grace and favour,
all serve our purpose.

The furnace in fruit, the infinite
repetitions of water, the slow eruption
of the chestnut's bright bolus,
all serve our purpose.

There's brightness in every cell;
we designed a vast hive.

We are the pioneers,
the frontiersmen.
We are the engineers,
the husbandmen.

David Harsent

Look at the sea. From the sea look back at the land -
this is the place you were meant to discover;
This is the place where everything went as planned.

What we have made will last forever.

from The Hoop of the World

Berts, Toms, Jacks & a Sig

[adaptation of a lecture first delivered to accompany an exhibition of paintings at All Saints Arts Centre, Lewes, East Sussex, 5th May 1996]

BERT Weedon, the popular guitar legend and author of the classic tutorial handbooks *Play in a Day* and *Guitarring! Learn to play the Weedon Way*. BERT, the legend has it, would appear on stage and at the climax of his concert would announce to his enthralled audience that he would play 200 notes in one minute. It's probably a minor quibble, but I've always instinctively felt that this display of technical virtuosity might have been even more remarkable if the 200 notes BERT played in that minute were not all of the same pitch.
As it was, the Weedon Way represents a striking example of what in artistic circles would be called an exaggerated emphasis of Form at the expense of Content.

BERTolt Brecht, offers this anecdote in a piece entitled *Form & Substance* from his collection *Tales from the Calendar:*

"Mr. K. contemplated a painting in which certain objects were given a very arbitrary form. He said:
'With some artists it's the same as with many philosophers when they look at the world. In striving for form, they lose the substance! I once worked for a gardener. He gave me a pair of shears and told me to clip a laurel bush. The bush grew in a tub and was hired out for festive occasions. So it had to be in the shape of a ball. I immediately set about cutting off the untidy shoots, but however hard and long I tried to make it ball shaped I did not succeed. First I trimmed too much off one side, then too much off the other. When at last it was a ball, it was a very small one. The gardener was disappointed and said: Yes that's a ball, but where's the laurel?"

The problem of form and content in art is an old and a vexed one. If Mr K's employer had been not a gardener but an exterior designer (if such things exist) of the modern movement, he might have clapped his protégé on the back, congratulated him on liberating the ordered perfection of the sphere from the chaotic tyranny of the bush, and ordered an extra pair of shears to complete the remainder of the operation. The two avant-gardeners might then have sat down on their laurels, tuned their spherical bakelite transistor radio to the minimalist's wavelength and relaxed to a live recital by maestro BERT Weedon.

What Mr K. had encountered is this old problem of Form and Content. "When the thing represented is at one with the manner of representing it" wrote Van Gogh to his brother Theo, "isn't it just that which makes a work of art good." R B Kitaj represents form and content as two figures whose relationship is ambiguous - they could be locked in combat, could be locked in an embrace. And that is the reality of the situation. The illusion is that the two can be discussed separately.

A couple of months ago, when I was asked to submit a lecture for this festival, the unavoidable pressures of advance publicity meant that I had to decide on a title before I had chance to think of a subject. A bit like being handed a free rein without being told what sort of beast your reins are attached to. *Carte blanche*, on the condition that it's put before the horse. This state of affairs in some way explains the faintly bizarre title, for which I now apologise. BERTs, TOMs, JACKs and a Sig. The basic idea, as I recall, was that it sounded meaningless enough to enable me, when the time came, which it has, to ramble on about pretty much whatever I like. Well what I *am* going to ramble on about is Making Things Make Sense. My work as an artist and writer has (I realise now) to a large extent been concerned with The Urge to Make Things Make Sense. And it is the *Urge* -which is great - rather than the Sense - which is minimal - which in the end makes things make sense.
And since I am now trying to reconcile that with BERTs, TOMs, JACKs and a Sig, this old problem of form and content seems a good enough place to start.

I am indebted to Stefan Themerson (*Logic, Labels and Flesh,* 1974) for the following observation: Imagine a big chunk of Carrara marble. For a physicist its weight would mean a downward force due to the earth's gravitational pull (and equal, though opposite, of the upward force exerted on it by whatever it stands on). Our physicist may express this by writing it like this:

$$1000K \times 9.8 \, (m/sec2)$$

The expression refers to the particular piece of marble, situated on Earth, near sea level. But he can go further. He can generalise. He can write something like this:

$$K\left(\frac{m_1 \times m_2}{d^2}\right)$$

This new expression, this formula, will refer not only to our particular chunk of Carrara marble and the Earth, it will refer to the gravitational pull of two men on opposite sides of the equator, or that of two electrons on opposite sides of BERT Einstein's universe. Yet this is not the end of the story. What he can do now is give his formula to a pure mathematician, who doesn't care a damn about Carrara marble, men on the equator, or electrons, and will rarefy the formula further still by expressing it in pure squiggles, which refer to nothing at all except themselves and show nothing but pure form. It can be said now that the physicist's first expression was the form of which the Carrara marble (or what he knew about it) was the content, that his second expression was the form of which the first expression was the content, and so on. Thus we have a series, such that on one end of it there is a 'material', perceivable content, whose form becomes the content of a more rarefied form, which becomes the content of.. .&c., till we arrive at the pure form, distilled by the mathematician.

Now, all this seems to be precisely the other way around with the artist. Assuming that the chunk of Carrara marble is made into a sculpture, for him it, the perceivable, seeable, touchable piece of matter, will be the form in which some content, say *David*, has been expressed. Yet this content, an Israelite shepherd boy bearing a sling, is itself a form into which a more general content has been personified:

Youth and the spirit of conquest. And this again is a form expressing some content even more general, still further stripped of accidentals, 'deeper', not to say 'metaphysical'.

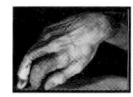

Thus here, in the artist's studio, we seem to have a reversed order. On one end of the series, a 'material', palpable, visible form which expresses a content that is the form of a more concentrated content, which is the form of…&c., till we arrive at a pure, unverbalised, non-physical content, embedded somewhere in the 'heart' of the sculptor.

The reversal is intriguing. Some artists have found it intriguing enough to attempt to see art in the way which is commonly held to be the scientist's way of seeing the world. By considering their raw material as the content.

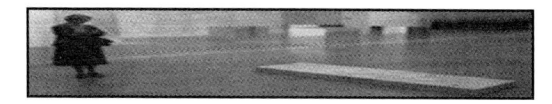

So the Form and Content problem is a complicated one. And as we look closer, a number of mechanisms seem to be at work simultaneously here. The appearance of a new artistic content provokes the appearance of a new artistic form.

The appearance of a new form stimulates the creation of another. Art historians account for developments in art by referring to changes in the environment. Technological changes, social changes, political and economic changes introduce new experiences which penetrate and shape the vocabulary of an artist. The new vocabulary brings with it it's own internal 'formal' problems.

I've quoted BERTolt Brecht, now I'll quote another BERT· RoBERT Hughes, from *The Shock of the New*:

'The speed at which culture reinvented itself through technology in the last quarter of the nineteenth century and the first decades of the twentieth century, seems almost preternatural. What emerged from the growth of scientific and technical discovery, as the age of steam passed into the age of electricity, was the sense of an accelerated rate of change in all areas of human discourse, including art. From now on the rules would quaver, the fixed contours of knowledge fail under the pressure of new experience and the demand for new forms to contain it."

But the interlocking of form and content is yet more complicated because, after a time, new forms tend to become content, just as a form of government, for example, Democracy, introduced in one generation, may become the very content of political thinking for the next one, demanding again a new, sometimes perplexingly surprising, form in which to express itself.

In artistic terms, it is worth considering that Michelangelo - for whom the human form became the vehicle to express an idealised content of harmony, balance and Humanism -

would have been utterly incapable of comprehending the late self-portraits of Rembrandt.

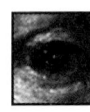

Because for Rembrandt, Humanity was no longer the form, it had become his content. Hence his exploration of all its attendant tragedy and frailty.

To make things more complicated still, the old content itself may become a form. Cezanne and Van Gogh invented new forms to express some old content. The content of Cezanne's views of Mont St Victoire are at least as old as the geological accident that is the landscape of Provence;

Van Gogh's *Church at Auvers* is as old as, well, the church at Auvers. It was Cezanne's form that became the content for Picasso and Braque

whose own form architectured of shifting planes and facets built around a disjointed cubist grid, in turn became the content of, amongst others, Mondrian's abstraction.

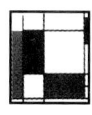

And it was Van Gogh's form that became the content for Kandinsky's spontaneous improvisations with point, line, plane and colour

whose form eventually becomes the content of an anti-formalist abstraction which is the content that ate the form that lay in the house that JACKson Pollock built.

John Berger, writing in 1960 about JACKson Pollock's exuberant *Blue Poles* painted less than a decade before, claimed: "These pictures are meaningless. But the way in which they are so is significant."

Responsive as I am to the writing of John Berger, something inside me has nevertheless always rebelled against this widespread critical reception of JACKson Pollock's drip-paintings as meaningless. Even despite Pollock's own oft-quoted refrain that "It just is!", I find myself refusing to accept that these enthralling, lavish, courageous, iconoclastic and, genuinely impressive paintings are without meaning. I do accept that they are, perhaps, *incomprehensible*, in the literal sense of the word as ununderstandable. (Although, even this I accept somewhat in the spirit of TOM Carlyle when somebody told him that Harriet Martineau, a devout Unitarian, had 'accepted the universe' and he said "By God, she'd better!") But, even given that it may not be *understandable* in verbal terms, it doesn't necessarily follow that the painting has no meaning. Words are not the one and only raw material to use for conveying meaning. Johann Sebastian Bach creates and conveys something about the world which is meaningful and yet is neither made in words nor can one convey it in words. And so do song thrushes. And humpback whales.

Another BERT - GilBERT Ryle, in *The Concept of The Mind*, asks (and I think he asks it rhetorically):
"Does it matter if all attempts at giving a hard-edged definition of 'meaning' break down somewhere or other?"

At this point I would like to give a definition of my own. Not of *meaning* but of what I think an artist is. Even though I have at the back of my mind - and as I write it's racing up to the front of my mind - a memory of just such a definition proposed by the Dada artist Tristan Tzara for the benefit of a sceptical British consul in TOM Stoppard's 1975 play *Travesties*.

This is how (with a little paraphrasing) TOM Stoppard's Tristan Tzara auto-defined himself:

"Doing the things by which is meant Art" (he says) "is no longer considered the proper concern of the artist. In fact it is frowned upon. Besides which I wouldn't know how to do them anyway. No, nowadays, an artist is someone who makes Art mean the things he does. A man may be an artist by exhibiting his hindquarters. He may be a poet by drawing words out of a hat, in fact some of my best poems have been drawn out of my hat which I afterwards exhibited to general acclaim at the Dada gallery in Bahnhofstrasse. And if you point out that I have simply changed the meaning of the word Art, then…good. I am pleased that I have made myself clear."

"Then you are not actually an *artist* at all?" Says the baffled Consul.

"On the contrary" replies Tzara, "I have just told you that I am."

Well, that might go some way to describing Tristan Tzara. It travels a bit farther still as a definition of Dada, since it hits that blind stroke of incoherence and self-contradiction that was the heroic hallmark of Dada. ('To be against the Dada Manifesto', shouted the Dada Manifesto, 'is to be a Dadaist!') But as a general definition of the artist, I'd have to say it isn't a watertight case.

Something that TOM Stoppard's conservative British Consul immediately recognised:

"But that does not make you an artist" (he replies to Tzara) "An artist is someone who is gifted in some way that enables him to do something more or less well which can only be done badly or not at all by someone who is not thus gifted. If there is any point in using language at all it is that a word is taken to stand for a particular fact or idea and not for other facts or ideas. I might claim to be able to fly. ..Lo, I say, I am flying. 'But you are not propelling yourself about while suspended in air', someone might point out. Ah no, I reply, that is no longer considered the proper concern of people who can fly. In fact it is frowned upon. Nowadays, a flyer never leaves the ground and wouldn't know how. I see, says my somewhat baffled interlocutor, so when you say you can *fly* you are using the word in a purely private sense. I see I have made myself clear, I say. Then, says this chap in some relief; you cannot actually fly after all? On the contrary, I say, I have just told you I can."

My simple proposal for a definition of an artist. Any artist. And I would further suggest this as the defining feature that distinguishes the Artist from the Illustrator. It is, quite simply this: that an artist might be defined by the fact that when he or she makes a mark on canvas, or on paper, or on a computer screen, or on whatever surface he or she chooses to make his or her mark, that (s)he is aware of entering into and participating in an ongoing debate about the relationship of those marks to the rest of the visual and philosophical world that goes right back to the first scratchings on the cave walls.

I propose that plaintive definition as a way of combating this claim that JACKson Pollock's painting *Blue Poles* is meaningless. Indeed, in the specific case of Pollock, I am convinced that to regard him in those terms is to recognise not only his great significance and contribution as an artist but also to excavate the intrinsic 'meaning' of his work. Now this may seem an eccentric manoeuvre - to search for the meaning of a painting, not by analysing the painting, but by examining the artist. But I'm not at all sure that it is as unreasonable as it sounds.

BUTTUCKS PTOE BUTES

This might be a fragment of poetry dredged from Tristan Tzara's hat. In which case it's meaning lies in it's meaninglessness. Because of course non-sense is the means by which Dada made sense of the world. If, however, we make the assumption that this is *not* the work of a Dadaist, and it *does* carry a meaning that is intelligible and communicable, wouldn't it be legitimate to try and find it not by analysis of the text, but by looking into the typewriter that produced it? And thus discovering empirically that its letters **p,o**, and **l** had got interchanged with **b, u** and **t.**

POLLOCKS BLUE POLES

The point I'm attempting to ambush here is that it isn't the way in which Pollock's paintings are meaningless that makes them significant, it is the way in which they are significant - historically, artistically, and (if you happen to be a dealer, collector or auctioneer) economically - that makes them make sense, that makes them, quite literally, drip with meaning.
I've been careful so far to avoid, or even at times to subvert any too direct disclosure of what I think I am doing as a painter or as an artist.

Drew Hewitt

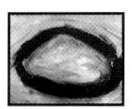

This is a painting I made 3 years ago. Its title is *Untitled.* I'm not going to commit the *folie de grandeur* of attempting to verbalise a non-verbal process, nor of trying to convince you that any opinions or interpretations I may have formed about my work in retrospect have any relevance at all to the way I approached the work or will approach any future work. It is my firm conviction that the work springs less from *what* I think about than the *way* I think about it.

I have two other authorities on my side here - two more BERTs - first, David HerBERT Lawrence's warning:

'Trust the tale, not the teller.'

Then, hopping briefly back to the physicist's laboratory, AlBERT Einstein:

"If you want to find out anything from theoretical physicists about the methods they use" he advised, "I advise you to stick closely to one principle: Don't listen to their words, fix your attention on their deeds."

A moment ago, I proposed a simple formalist definition of what I think an artist is, by suggesting what I think an artist *does.* Or rather, what I think an artist thinks when he does it. I proposed this definition as a means to ambush some meaning which I instinctively, or intuitively, or intellectually felt to be in a particular work of art. What you might call the inherent truth of that work of art. I didn't feel it was necessary to embark upon the hopeless and, indeed, pointless task of attempting to define *Art* in order to isolate the meaning of an art work.

Let's, for a moment, jump back a bit to BERT Brecht's Mr. K. who was, you might remember, contemplating 'a painting in which certain objects were given a very arbitrary form.' He said: "With some artists it's the same as with many philosophers when they look at the world. In striving for form, they lose the substance."

Again, I acknowledge a debt to Stefan Themerson for pointing out (in the introduction to his volume on *Semantic Poetry*) that there have been two recent schools of philosophy which have attempted to isolate meaning through definition. The first one, to put it as shortly, and as obscurely, as possible, professed that *the truth of the semiotic is in its pragmatics*. In other words, that the entire meaning of any intellectual conception is in its practical consequences. In other words, that the truth of a proposition is to be judged by its results. For instance: the meaning of a statement that something is funny is in the fact that people will laugh. And the meaning of such a thing as a ball-shaped laurel bush is in the fact that song thrushes no longer consider it a suitable home to rear their young.

Alas, this philosophy, useful as it is in defining some concepts, seems to be useless when we try to define some other concepts, such concepts, for instance, as: Art. Indeed if somebody asked *me* to define what Art is; what it is I think I do as an artist, by enumerating its *pragmatic* consequences and *praxeological* usefulness, the best thing I could do would be to quote that great inventor, TOM Alva Edison. The story goes that, when he was demonstrating his new gadget, the phonograph, somebody said to him: "It's marvellous, Mr Edison, but what is the use of it?", Edison answered: "And what is the use of the newborn child?"

The other, equally modern philosophy, began with another TOM. St TOM the Apostle. The doubting TOM (who is, for me, incidentally, the real hero of the New Testament. Forget the miracle worker, this is your man). It was he who said:
"Except I shall see in his hands the prints of the nails, and put my finger into the prints of the nails, and thrust my hand into his side, I will not believe."

This anti-irrationalist philosophy, to put it again as shortly, and as obscurely, as possible, starts by professing that *the truth of the semiotic is in its semantics.* In other words: that the analysis of language shows that it is futile to try to say what can only be shown. In other words: that (except in logic and mathematics) - meaningful statements are only those which can be verified by sense experience. Stefan Themerson *(ibid.)* asks: "Can you define Love as you define things in algebra? Can you hear Time as you can hear a cuckoo clock? And can you touch Sorrow as you can touch a rose petal?"

And to which I add: Can you smell Art as you can smell oil paint and turpentine?

A moment ago, I quoted TOM Alva Edison and TOM the Apostle. Let me now quote two other TOMs. When people asked TOM Aquinas what is Time, he answered:
"So long as you don't ask me, I know. As soon as I'm asked, I don't."
And when they asked TOM a Kempis what is Contrition, he said:
"I would rather feel it than be able to define it."

Now, I know that plenty of non-sense has been said by theologians (and I'll come to that in a moment) -on the other hand, plenty of sense has *not* been said by both linguistic and the physicistic philosophers. And so if I were asked again to try and define Art, what it is that I am doing as an artist, I could only say: "So long as you don't ask me, I know. As soon as I'm asked, I don't. But I would rather feel it than be able to define it."

Drew Hewitt

In Caravaggio's painting, St. TOM the Apostle. The doubting TOM is depicted at the moment of thrusting his hand into the side of Christ, which is, as I have just mentioned, the moment at which he predicted he would believe.

Now, I wonder if that *believe* is the same *believe* that BERT Einstein meant when he said to Gustave Ferrière: "I don't believe in mathematics".

Or is it the sort of *believe* that Einstein meant when, in the week ending 5th April 1953, he earned himself a place in the *Observer*'s 'Sayings of the Week' column by saying "I cannot believe that God plays dice with the cosmos."

Now, I don't know what it is in me that revolts against this word *believe*, but I do know that I object to it on deeper grounds than most of the people who use it. And I am still somewhat surprised by the strength of my rebellion against using this word. I don't think I believe, or ever believed, but I've certainly bored many people with my fierce aversion to the word *belief*. And, since I now have a captive audience, I fully intend to bore a few more.

At first I thought it was a personal foible. I've even traced it back to an incident in my childhood when I remember a woman confessing to my mother that she didn't believe in gas cookers. Well even at the age of five or six years old, I was suspicious of the basis for her disbelief. For a start, I was aware of the accumulated evidence of several dozen gas cookers of my own acquaintance, squatting in kitchens in my own neighbourhood, that were heavily weighted against her faith. And it worried me, this woman's blindness. It worried me no less than the people I witnessed to-ing and fro-ing from church on a Sunday. Their belief was as mysterious and as ludicrous to me, as blindly oblivious of the facts, as this woman's professed non-belief.

It's not uncommon, I suspect, for the atheistic mind to become so inspired by the mystery of belief. Believers of different Faiths tend, like magnetic poles of a similar persuasion, to instinctively repel. But the Unbeliever and the Faithful are all North and South. The fascination is mutual and irresistible. The force is so compelling that hapless evangelists drawn ineluctably to my doorstep have eventually to contrive desperately elaborate excuses to leave. An involuntary mental analogy of the scene tends to gatecrash my mind on such occasions: an image of an eager David Attenborough sort of figure, safari-suited and whispering in earnest. Hacking through dense forest he suddenly stumbles upon a clearing where rests a full-grown gorilla, chewing on a tree trunk. Inspired by the broad grin that the gorilla returns to him, the determined missionary courageously but cautiously dips a hand into his haversack and produces... a banana! Which he tentatively proffers across this vast anthropoid divide, oblivious to the fact that (a) gorillas don't actually eat bananas and (b) gorillas actually eat people.

Whether you insert yourself into the safari suit, the gorilla suit, or you observe the scene crouched down in the surrounding undergrowth with the rest of the camera team - I like to think of that as a reasonable barometric indication of your level of belief, atheism or agnosticism.

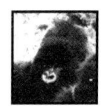

It's not that I object to the notion of belief *per se*. Not at all. What I find myself objecting to is the blithe substitution of knowledge with belief. Let me explain.
You can *know* (either because you were taught so, or learnt it by experience) that if you turn to the next page of this book, the text will continue in the accustomed manner left to right across the line; lines running from top to bottom on the page; and you can *believe* that if you turn to the next page of this book, the text will continue in the accustomed manner - left to right across the line; lines running from top to bottom on the page. If you *know,* and then it happens that the words on the next page are scrambled into incoherence, you might study the arrangement of words and set about unscrambling some order from the chaos, or you might curse the technology responsible for this unfortunate error in print production and demand a satisfactory replacement from the publisher or bookseller. But if you had *believed*: if you had *believed*, then you should have to go down on your knees, or put your hat on, or touch the floor with your forehead and pray forgiveness from the publisher (or the book) for the sins with which you must have offended this publication, even if you didn't know when or how you committed them. To say that you *know* a thing to be true is also to embrace the possibility of that thing *not* being true. Beliefs cannot be true or not true. They can only be firm or not so firm, deep or not so deep.

Drew Hewitt

I might *know* that there have only been two great Irish painters And I might *know* them to be JACK B Yeats.

And JACK O'Metty

And sooner or later, probably accompanied by a considerable degree of embarrassment, I will revise my list of the great Irish painters, and strike off the latter of those names. But if I had *believed* that the only two great Irish artists were JACK B Yeats and JACK O'Metty, then even when the evidence of the latter's Swiss citizenship came to my attention, I would be bound not to let myself become convinced by it, I would have to think that the whole world was wrong and only I was right, I would have to invent a faked biography for JACK O'Metty to suit my belief and I would have to come to the conclusion that an evil conspiracy was being waged by heretics to exile O'Metty from the emerald shores of his Mother Ireland.

And that is what believers do. And they must do so. For, if they really believe, whether in Transubstantiation or in mathematics or in dice-throwing deities, they know that once they allow their faith to be destroyed by evidence brought forward on Monday, Wednesday may bring new evidence which will destroy what they believed on Tuesday. The brutality and suffering that we see every day in the world around us could serve as evidence against the assumption of God's beneficence. But, if one believes in His goodness, one prefers to forget His omnipotence, and invents devils, and original sin. And not even the intellectually spurious get-out clause of Free Will excuses the overwhelming evidence to show that excess of suffering and poverty warps a person's character. But, if one believes, one prefers to borrow the idea of purification.

The statement that the Earth is the *centrum mundi* was at one time *truth* for those who (however erroneously) *knew* it; and at the same time *prejudice* for those who *believed* it. For the former the system originally suggested by Copernicus but further elaborated by Galileo was a great discovery, a revelation, illuminating and unknotting the complicated net of the Ptolemean system; for the latter, for the believers, it was a terrible revolutionary shock. The only possible outcome of which was that Galileo should be persecuted as a heretic, because the believers were bound not to let themselves become convinced by the evidence of a slowly swinging 25 kg copper ball (which for the last 125 years has been slowly swinging from the ceiling of a twelfth century church in France) proving to anyone who cares to observe it's ponderous swaying that the Earth does indeed turn on its axis. The device is called *Foucault's Pendulum*.

And it gives me the opportunity to bring on board another BERT.

UmBERTo Eco's novel *Foucault's Pendulum* opens with an aphoristic paradox: 'Superstition brings bad luck' which is appropriate here if only because it reminds me of another of TOM Stoppard's observations, this time from his 1988 play *Hapgood* and this time concerning the Danish theorist, Niels Bohr, seen here with BERT Einstein.

'Niels Bohr lived in a house with a horseshoe on the wall. When people cried, for God's sake, Niels, surely *you* don't believe a horseshoe brings you luck!, he said, no, of course not, but I'm told it works even if you don't believe it."

BERTrand Russell, in *An Inquiry into Meaning and Truth:* adds his voice to the debate: "Belief", he says "does not need a justification from reason. To say: I believe because I know x is true, is as much a hysterical confusion as to say: I feel pain because I know that sharp knives hurt, or: I love because I know that people who kiss love."

On the contrary, there is no contradiction, but perfect clarity in Shakespeare's distinction between 'I know' and 'I believe'.

"When my love swears that she is made of truth.
I do believe her, though I know she lies".

'I believe' describes what exists in the mind; 'I know' describes what exists outside the mind. Which might be an end to the matter, if it weren't for one more BERT - GilBERT Keith Chesterton - the most endearingly rational of believers. In his volume of essays *Orthodoxy*, Chesterton discharges a round of return fire against the relentless volleys of the non-believers and then disarms the whole shooting match by pointing

Drew Hewitt

out, with impeccable reasoning, that:
"Reason is itself a matter of faith. It is an act of faith to assert that our thoughts have any relation to reality at all."

Renaissance perspective was a geometrical system for depicting the illusion of reality. We are so familiar with it now, that we hardly notice it. It works by accumulating all the available data and ordering it into a simplified relationship between eye, brain and object. And since it would be meaningless to suggest that perspective exists in the 'real' world, it is therefore an abstraction. It is a way of organising the world and imposing meaning upon it, of rescuing order from chaos. It is a way of making things make sense. In the particular case of renaissance perspective, visual things.

We construct other systems to make sense of other aspects of our experience. Some of our systems of thought are very elaborate and complex. And many alternative systems exist side by side, contemporary and contradictory: Creationism and Darwinism; Marxism and Capitalism; Christianity and Islamic fundamentalism; crime and punishment; war and peace; Vegetarianism and MacDonalds-ism. Other systems, as I outlined earlier, pass on, as it were, their DNA through a series of evolving generational mutations in form and content. Thus: Post-Impressionism becomes Abstract Expressionism; Ptolemean Astronomy becomes Galilean Astronomy; Newtonian Physics becomes Einsteinian physics.

The delicatessen counter that is Post-modernism has confused this situation even further by serving up as art and entertainment the pluralism that is at the heart of the system of systems that is our culture. We sample a full smorgasbord of gods and heroes where Apollo is a space rocket; Mars is a chocolate bar and Ajax, a cream cleanser. Without a hint of contradiction, Atheists experience their disbelief to the sounds of Bach's B Minor Mass, while celibate philosophers thrill to a dialectic filtered through Cilla's Blind Date.

All this makes the task of older, more established systems, like, for example, the Christian church that much harder to accomplish without constantly reinventing itself (which it does in both form and content), so that it might stand some chance of competing in a world that runs from Mr Blobby to Mrs Bobbit; a world of genetic engineering and birth control; of twin carburettors, Three-Mile Island, and four-minute milers; of hearing aids and band-aids, and marital aids and red lemonades; and AIDS…

Now I don't mean to suggest that the Church's insistence on constantly underpinning it's own foundations makes its task any less purposeful, or even less meaningful. The Forth Road Bridge isn't invalidated as a structure just because it has to be repainted every four years. Just because Westminster Abbey needs a damn good clean once in a while, there's no necessity to call in the demolition men. Putting that spiky word *belief* to one side for a moment - the Hand of God, whether you take it to be waving or drowning, may be less conspicuous now; curing leprosy may no longer be the preserve of the miracle worker, and turning water into wine may not now constitute a certificate of Messiah-ship, but the agonies of life are eased not by double-sprung mattresses and physiotherapy.

It seems worth noting here that whereas the Church's various recent attempts to renew itself have largely been concerned with rectifying the yawning abyss between the rich complexity and exquisite precision of its *form* (its elaborate manner of presentation through ritual, language and dress) and the ludicrously ill-considered banality and vagueness of its *content*[1] ; the scientific community, on the other hand, has in recent years attempted to renew *it*self by way of a reverse manoeuvre. *It* has traditionally suffered from an exaggerated emphasis on *content* at the negligence of *form*. Bring to mind, if you will, Open University television broadcasts of the 1970's; the corduroy-suited, kipper-tied, tousle bearded, stammering apology at the blackboard, and gaze across to the vertiginous Grand Canyon that separated the ludicrously ill-considered banality and vagueness of this manner of presentation from the rich complexity and exquisite precision of the scientific information it proposed.

What I'm circling here (like a salivating vulture impatiently wheeling beneath a baking sun) is the way in which we make things make sense. By viewing selected data in a selective way, meanings emerge, or more accurately: meanings are produced. The data thus viewed act as clues to meaning. Of course, look at the same clues from a different perspective, you get a different set of solutions, a different meaning.

---

1. Vivian Stanshall: "Strange how the mumbo jumbo of the Catholic Latin Mass stopped making sense when they started doing it in a language we could understand."

Many years ago, the enclosed free gift designed to entice me as a young breakfaster to a pack of Kellogg's Frosties (as if I needed enticing) was a *Codebreaker*. A *Codebreaker* was a cardboard envelope with holes punched, randomly it seemed, in one side, and another rectangle of card on which was printed a grid within which were arranged, randomly it seemed, letters of the alphabet. The card was slipped into the envelope which, obscuring some of the letters and revealing others, created a message. And if the card was rotated and then inserted into the envelope, different letters were obscured, different letters revealed, a different message resulted. The *Codebreaker* was thus a simple selective filtration system for creating a kind of order from a sort of chaos. It is an innocent example, but it strikes me now that it was the form of the *Codebreaker,* its filtration system, rather than the content of the messages so revealed, that has proved memorable.

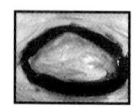

Our own personally designed filtration systems sift our own personal versions of order from the chaos around us. I have used as my embarkation point a highly selective filtration system of BERTs TOMs and JACKs. There is a Frenchman (he is called Jacques but prefers to go by the *nom de guerre* of Monsieur Mangetout) who has, to date, *eaten* seven bicycles, a supermarket trolley, six television sets, a vacuum cleaner, two brass beds and a Cessna 150 four-seater light aircraft. That is how he makes the world make sense. Sometimes it's easier to do it by means of such highly unselective, and only slightly more digestible filtration systems as multi-channel television or newspaper editors. Whatever way we choose, these structures we build and use to unscramble the world - what I have referred to as *form* - are no less integral to meaning than the *content* they yield.

Earlier on I resisted any attempt to try and define Art. Try it and you immediately become aware of the things that the description leaves out. Better to say what is *Art* than what *Art* is. But it does strike me that what artists do do, is make connections, they link things together. A final TOM - the Victorian poet Francis Thompson. He was the son of a Roman Catholic Doctor and was intended for the priesthood, but was judged not to have a vocation. He also failed to qualify as a doctor, so rather splendidly failed his father on both counts. He consequently left home to spend three years of homeless and opium-addicted destitution in London. This is from his poem *The Mistress of Vision*:

>When to the new eyes of thee
>All things by immortal power,

Near or far,
Hiddenly,
To each other linkèd are
That thou canst not stir a flower
Without trembling a star.

Sigmund Freud. He'd have had Francis TOMpson on his couch in a trice. Freudian theory is a system - I think it is a very elegant, economical and beautifully designed system - for making connections. It has its deficiencies of course. Particularly if you suffer from what Freud seemed to think was the biological misadventure of being female. And I sincerely doubt its value as a therapeutic tool. But that, for me at least, and until I have need of a psychoanalyst, isn't actually the point. It may have been for Freud, but it's not for me. I am willing to count myself a Freudian purely on my admiration of the elegance of its formal design, and for the rather enjoyable quirk that, in its practical application as Psychoanalysis, it does, quite literally set out to make things make sense. Though in this case, the things are people.

It seems to me that it is some sort of indication of the persuasiveness of Freudian theory as an ideology and it seems preferable to think of ideologies as more or less persuasive, rather than more or less 'truthful' - that it has, in the twentieth century, become so pervasive; what Auden called 'a climate of thought'.

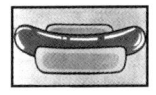

I tried to capture a flavour of this climate in a screenplay for a feature film entitled *Come Again.* A Freudian psychoanalyst has in his consulting room a tramp who claims, maybe even *believes,* that he comes from the planet Venus. After a few minutes of analysis, the tramp erupts in a tirade against his analysand:

"You have made the world obscene, your type! Your method of cleaning up minds is simply to make them as dirty as your own. Back on my planet, it is the custom for female Venusians to have intercourse with their eldest son, after which she changes into a man. The successor becomes the predecessor. That's why up there our mathematics is different, and down here things don't add up. It all makes for a pretty messy family tree, but it's what makes our little blue world go round.
    And then I come down here. Amongst you earthlings. In a spirit of interplanetary bonhomie. And people like you implant into my mind your concept of Oedipus. Now

Drew Hewitt

I can no longer entertain homely thoughts of my poor Mama without blushing. And it doesn't stop there! No! There was a time when I could enjoy the beautiful sight of your tellurian waves crashing onto your tellurian rocks with the innocent and wondrous eyes of a newcomer. Now I sit atop Lulworth Cove and I cannot see for tears. You have affected my pure Venusian intellect to the point that I cannot contemplate the view anymore without my vision becoming infected by the most obscene metaphorical discharge. I look to the sea and I find that fish fail to swim and oysters no longer harbour pearls without arousing in me the most disturbing suggestion of impropriety. I look inland: worms have ceased to burrow through soil and I cannot watch rhubarb push its head through the earth without a deep sense of shame.

And don't tell me the problem is inside my head, because it's in *all* our heads! And that makes it out there! And by telling people to abandon their feelings of shame, you are just abandoning responsibility. You are fiddling with yourself while romance burns! This is a modern epidemic, overtaking your planet! Open the window! Look out there on the streets! Women are afraid to put rings on their fingers and their fingers in their purses. Grown men have developed a phobic reaction to eating bananas in public. Don't you see! You haven't just burst the bubble - you have pricked it, penetrated it and left it flaccid! There was a time when decent people had intercourse to put sex out of their minds. Now, their minds are so stuffed with it, their heads so throbbing with it that when men sneeze they inadvertently pull out curry-flavoured contraceptives from their handkerchief pockets! And their isn't a hole they can hide their heads in that won't condemn them!"

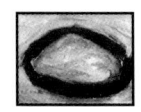

It has also been rather intriguingly noted recently that Freudianism as a formal structure, can be seen as a mutation of some much older content, as good old Judaic Christian theology dressed up in new medical and technical clothes; that all Freud really did was to translate a religious content into a form that would suit his atheism, by repackaging the doctrine of original sin, the idea that we're all split, with a higher self, the soul, and a base or animal half.

Just as Christianity proclaimed we're all damned through our base half, so Freud proclaims we're all in thrall to the untamed desires of infant sexuality and the unconscious. Christianity tells us we can reach spiritual enlightenment and righteousness through the church and prayer; Freud tells us it's via the couch, five days a week.

And you can even take Freud as a sort of Messiah, though not many do. But all the parallels are there: analysis replaces the confessional - the analyst as the silent remote

God of Protestantism, listening inscrutably to the outpourings of the believer.

And this analogy can be carried yet further, into the general spirit of scientific inquiry. The unconscious angel/beast division isn't unique to psychoanalysis, it was right there at the heart of the Puritan Enlightenment. And now it can be discerned running right through the scientific method. Out go feelings, subjectivity and the emotions, while reason and the mind take charge.
Original sin is being kept artificially alive in a cage in the laboratory.

Please release me. As EngelBERT would say.

Old Man River

(For JW, In Memoriam)

I

Old man at the end of his years. The mud. Last house on the river the end of town. The mud. Staring across to the opposite bank. Old man upon his verandah. The last of the daylight. Ball of liquid golden fire being suckt into a blue grey blanket. Glorious as per usual. Old man at the end. The Ouse at low ebb. Fresh thick stench and salt air and the shrill sharp clamour of a few passing gulls. Glorious as per usual. How measure, how weigh, how comprehend the sum of one's years, the stuff of one's life? Old man upon his verandah staring across to the mudbank opposite. Transfixt. Thick wet mud. Shelves of thick wet putrefied slop. Shit brown viscid mass pockt and splattered. A limed urinous slime oiled by the light. The oozing banks of the Ouse. Oiled and shiny in the last of the sunlight. Glorious as per usual. Tufted by coarse grey grass. Grey green grass. That arc of fire that burned over the castle ruins, throwing the town, the hill, into silhouette, now sunken into a smouldering dull grey wash. The dying of the light. Seventy seven summers is not so many. Not so very many. Old man at the last of his having. How fast the rise and fall of the river. The ebbing away of one's days. The ebbing away of this day. Light dying upon his verandah. Staring across to the other side. The mud.

II

Last house on the Ouse the end of town. Last town on the Ouse before the sea. Here he: an old man transfixt. Upstream the river a screen of rippling light. A current of flashing whites and pinks under a pale translucent expanse. Horizon aglow still with the fizzing gore of the setting sun. Blue mudbanks a-glisten with silvery white wet light. A transcendental image. Downstream the contrary. Cloud without break. Dirty blue grey underbelly of cloud without break. Huge drifting cumulus limbs overlaid masse en masse. The river a darkening dense green. No reflection. The reflection of no light. Or next to no light. Mud the colour of mud. Down the river of years, down the river of years to this day of judgement. Last house under a divided sky. Old man at the court of wonder dumbstruck. How measure, how weigh, how comprehend? Seventy-seven times round that ball of fire. The mud. The light. The end.

Purgations
III

That other
That elusive other

How get close?
How realise that other?

One proceeds from definition to definition
Each definition making the next one possible

Like footsteps
Each step a clearing of the way through the blur

The clumsy swaddling of the mind peeled away layer by layer, bit by bit
The image of a hand in thick gloves, desperate to touch yet unable to feel

Then under these thick gloves there are other gloves and under these other
                                                            gloves other gloves
Each subsequent glove of a slightly finer texture than the previous

The progress of the understanding
The desire to touch with a naked hand

Mark C. Hewitt

Purgations
X

Snout in the humus rooting for truffles
The way that can be spoken of is not the constant way

One picks a thing up, perhaps captivated by its surface sheen, perhaps
                              considering that it will one day prove useful
Then when the thing proves useless, if the thing proves useless, or its sheen
                              wears off, if its sheen wears off, it is discarded

So many things pickt up and discarded
And so it is, that if one is ever to acquire it, then sick and tired at last of the
                            picking up and the getting rid, one acquires discernment

Nose
The cultivation of a nose

Trail of crap along the way
Snout in the humus rooting for truffles

Purgations
XII

Fantastic folly built from scratch in the wilderness
Bit by bit, brick by brick, year by year

Walls bejewelled with gewgaws, nick-nacks, bits of this, bits of that
Things pickt up along the way

Ridiculous ramshackle edifice thus, teetering in the wind
A monument to strife: lopsided and rough and messy

But mine, all mine
The triumph of endurance over despair

dear sir, congratulations
your strange and improbable erection has won third prize in our UK Year of the Mad
Fucker competition

yours to cherish, a lifetime's supply of red herrings
Nightmare! nightmare!

Mark C. Hewitt

102   Pierre Hollins

The Woman who mistook her Father for an Irishman

He was an upright man, a too-tight man
a man of honour, a man of blight, a sight
of land, a one-man band, a sweet tobacco
curling in the wool of his all-English coat.

He ruled, he puffed, he parked the car
in twenty jolts and shifts, he lifts the
load, adds up the profit, calculates the loss
and doesn't give a toss for her undoing.

Looking-after, she remembers, meant a window-seat,
a pleated curtain, knives of bone, a battle won,
taut strings, an overview, the one who always knew
the globe's best shape, its politics, its scars.

But when they watched the old films flicker, he
and his daughter, from the old plush seats that creak
with laughter; when Chaplin's tickle inches up
the legs and hits the belly hard and rattles there

and when they buckle into raucous groans
her father toppling headlong from his chair
is no more English than this lilt, this flare
of fiery sound that whips the heart to bits.

Then he's a tramp, a man whose song assaults
the Irish sea with unrequited love, until
the old gods tell him who he is and she can
recognise a rakish eye, a fiddler buried deep

and so far down her father's Irish heart is cleft
and hidden in his tweed, his socks, his tread
the rumbling of his wanton dreams in bed
the air's hiss as he draws a breath of music

through his pipe, in the mean time of the year,
the catch of breath flaring his pipe's bowl
like a crucible, nations welded in the ash
his daughter's heart a carbon copy of his own.

Nicki Jackowska

Marilyn on the Mountain

Imagine a pucker in the raw clay
of the mountain's lower slopes, as though
a woman lay just beneath the surface
and turning in her sleep, gives vent
to all her decades' longing,
the muddied turbulence of her desire.

You fall on your knees near to where her
mouth is, water-hole in rusting terra-cotta
the lips a fringe of tiny ribs, a bird's
last testament; as though the sand has
worried all its force against dead flesh
leaving a dove's bones finely represented
drawn as an artist might, pronouncing
his arrival at the gates of intervention.

The mouth sings its bullet straight at the eye.
Within that charcoaled cup there lurks
her tongue, caged like the lion she once was
and the dried ridges of her crusted pout
spread a parched and threadbare fan
upon the earth, that flickered once in halls
and drawing-rooms, coding her heart's intent.

So do the clues gather; a breathless fossil-wing
faint as poppies, an upper lip familiar
as grass, the lower falling like a suicide
painted by the sun's late copper glaze.
The orifice shapes an invitation dark as opium.
I kneel like a devotee, trysting with dust.
A lizard-man, branding my life to meet her,
perfect trick of wind, an artifice of weather.

I drool at the icon underneath, her lust.
A silk saliva-skin moistens the edges of
that hollow into luminescence; I lick her
out of tombs, roll back the film for evidence.
A hot pink duplication peppers the air,
whirrs like a newsreel in my eyes creating doves.
The kiss burns its flint, runs a lava-current
into the bag of bones suspended over her.

Far off, I taste the heat of canyons, gorges,
sweet cactus-flowers; until a coat of sand
scrapes at my throat's cave, and memory
scrambles like a crazy beggar among the stones
offering its kiss to every feature in the conspiracy
of pipe-dreams, parchment and the land's loose mould.

Entries on Light

1   Knocking on the door
   you open, after every
absence - yours or mine -
   as our grounds and elevations
realign themselves, you
   on the step below me, one
or both of the kids above
   I'm struck again as you
face me, turn your back, stricken
   by how small you are.

Bird mother, busy woodland
   creature mother
beginning-small and ending-small
   I don't believe that it's only
a kernel blown to husk
   the great revolve and vanishing-
point of our figures of eight
   as you cross the kitchen, lower
the gas and we, entering
   let the small shock pass

that is the shock: for
   watching your anxious steps
vanishing deep down corridors
   to return with gifts, it's more
with a sense of vastness, height
   that I see you shrink;
of radiance, like your candle
   lit in the daytime, that I notice
how pale your hair and skin seem
   beside ours.

2   Dwindling, as hollows
   deepen, brighten and what is
nearest catches light
   in the circle you inhabit and I

inherit, knowing my reach is smaller
　much too small to lift
and shawl you in my arms, fading
　you intensify, like candlelight
on scalloped lace, in the pink
　the very fabric of our lives.

First you invite me to tea under your appletree and now
　send me a photograph of where we sat, you, still ill
by your herbs in shade and I in a wedge of sun angled
　under apples. Let me not break the chain. Send you
a poem of your photo of the patio of your new home, wish you
　entirely better. The doorway's as narrow in its light
as shadow's broad and black in the kitchen. Blackest of all
　your bike in silhouette. And the appletree just visible
where bright light grows on a shrub I'd know, if it weren't
　for those clumps of flowering light you knew I'd like
has no flowers. But what can I write that's not in the eye?
　How something tall and narrow can suggest a yardage of sun
an L, one arm of which you'll plant, where drainpipes ask for disguise
　with shade-lovers? How, in a city's heart, Elephant & Castle
you can be in the heart of the country, how knee-high trellises
　fronting allotments whose tenants stop to talk to you, spell
an other worldliness? But you know all that. How memory
　speaks to the image, image to the word. How inadequate
we are in our borrowings, not knowing if by saying *I'm like you*
　we do violence. Thank you for the herbs, tea, the photo.
Think of this as a postcard but more than that, a short time
　spent in your company, after the event, a recognition of those
differences we run into now and then, alternatives we never chose -
　patios with loaded apple-trees, herb troughs, neighbouring
histories of architects and saints in the churches of south London;
　other people's knowledge vaguely interesting, vaguely boring
lifestyles, lovelives and sometimes even illnesses worn transparent
　on a face that brings it home: the equity no-one has in common;
differences that now and then make us feel are of less account
　than an hour or two - and I hate that word affirming but -
affirming, the way women do when we say *me too*, each other.
　(And the facings of your bookshelves like an opening accordion.)

Mimi Khalvati

In that childhood time
  of peering out
from a hut of leaves
  at the ebb and flow -

though little did
  sun perhaps on a glint
of straw, wind
  ballooning a shirt or branch -

each gust and pause, drift
  of skin between
warm and cold, was a source
  of mindless patience.

How a world could be
  changed from moment
to moment, broken
  by sudden entrances

a bumblebee, helicopter;
  resumed and our
solitude, brushing wings
  with its passing by

be, for the contact
  safer: this
was the ebb and flow
  we watched for

as though each shift of
  grass, flight of paper
float of shadow across a path
  weren't just earth's

response to a moving heaven
  but the heart's reply
shaping life
  and we its recording angel.

Mimi Khalvati

First Generation Monologue

Like every other Caribbean émigré
who'd put away the lamp of the sun
She spoke of the bad old migrant days:
I was in the ship's first wave.
No, I never realise it would have been
so cold and grey, so damp and dull
with all the buildings looking like
a prison-front, and even the dwelling
houses excluding my woman's walk;
the closed-up open shops. The fog.

Yes, it seemed as if the whole of England
was a Scrooge in those days of
four-people-living-in-a-room.
The smell of clothes, dank,
before the only heater.
The white landlady exact as the coin
clanking in the grudging meter.

I never forget the night
I got the news how Cousin Bernice negligée
catch fire while warming her foot
in front the paraffin heater on the floor;
how she run outside screaming into the cold:
Lord, Lord, to come all the way
to England, Bernice, a bright brown moth
just flickering out on the snow

Still I lighted my days
with memories blue as the indigo
of my mother's rinsing water.
I lighted on my memories
like a grasshopper.
Sometimes I was as stranded
as a salmon,

Grace Nichols

holding my fading hands
before the English fire.
How I longed for the openness of verandahs.

Eternity was greyness to me, I tell you,
the days I dragged myself across the days,
barely managing, snail-like
under that amorphous octopus of a sky.
The days I got my colours mixed -
a dream of colours -
on my brain's muddled palette;
Bright blue suddenly brushing grey aside,
slate-roofs glinting galvanise
and everywhere the shimmering
waves of heat,
Evergreens dripping
redblood blossoms at my feet.

Europe had become
part of my possession,
but how to come to terms
with the architecture?
The walls sealed and solid;
The closed door against the cold;
The ivy of my voice no longer
climbing towards the ceiling -
To overhang green and listening.

Where were my days
of leaning through windows,
parting the Trades?
Breezing out with Bo
in the shade of the backsteps,
dress lapped between legs like a river.

Loud ice in lemonade.
Bird-picked mangoes hiding in foliage.
Fowls grazing the backyard,
clean-neck, feather-neck,
each solitary;
eyes pulled down -
little photographic hoods
from the glare of the sun.
And Hibiscus, queen of all the flowers,
cupped red and rude against the paling,
still glistening with little mercuries
from the earlier shower of earthsmelling rain.
But never enough to keep us rooted.

Grace Nichols

Long-Man

(For Barbara Cole who first introduced us to the Long-Man, for Jan and Tim who came along and to The Druid Way by Philip Carr-Gomm)

On open downland we're as open as he -
Me and Jan, Tim and John,
Kalera and Ayesha,
And the cracked-sun
Has once again withdrawn.
Leaving us to windy shawls
And pewtery greys
To newly mowed down
Fecund-earth which the rains
Had furrowed into clay.

Plod-Plod
Through the caking-blood
Of England's sod,
Our good shoes growing
Sulkier by the minute,
As is my five-year-old,
Whose hand a sixth sense
Tells me to hold,
Despite her intermittent tugging
On this our hill-god pilgrimage.

And even when she manages
To break free, I'm after her,
A wiser Demeter -
Swiftfooted and heavy
With apprehension.
Sensing the weald-spirits
In a primitive pull
Of the pagan dimension.

'We're off to see
The Long-Man, the wonderful
Long-Man of Wilmington,'
I sing, humouring her over

The timeless witchery
Of the landscape.

Meanwhile, as always, he's there,
Looming out of the green coombe
Of Windover's womb.

In our heart-searching
And soul-yearning
We come to stand before him,
But soon our luminous eyes
Are nailing him with a
Crucifixion of questions -
Who and Why and How he came to be.
Male, Female, or ancient
Presage of a new androgyny?

With the sun back out
Surely he is benevolent
Corn-God and Shepherd
Of the good harvest?
Sun-in and he's
The Phantom-Symbol
Of all our foreboding.
The Gatekeeper-Reaper
Who would reap us in.
The faceless frozen traveller.
Moongazer.
Green Man-Mirror,
Tricking our eyeballs on -
The cunning chameleon.

But going back over
The wet green swelling
The presumptuous Goddess in me
Looks back and catches him -
Off guard.
Poor wounded man,
The staves in his arms
No barrier to a woman like
She-who-would-break-them
And take him in her arms.

Grace Nichols

The Holy Spirit

One summer afternoon in 1842 an extraordinary prisoner was brought in along the Brighton Road by Constable Martin. The man was dressed in a loose cheesecloth shirt and red sailor's trousers now little more than rags. Around his waist was kirtled a grubby blue silk sash. His whole appearance suggested destitution, but he rode beside the Constable in the police wagon, taking on the country scenery, as if in his own carriage on a royal progress. His arrest had taken place the previous day outside the Roman Catholic Chapel in Brighton, where he was seen begging from the communicants as they left the building after Sunday morning mass. Having spent the night in the police cells, the stranger had been summarily committed by the magistrate to one month's hard labour, and despatched under escort to Lewes Prison.

After some negotiation between the Porter and the Constable and an exchange of paperwork, the man, who could, in the Constable's view, understand but hardly speak English, was escorted by a turnkey into the receiving cell. This turnkey, Frederick Ancell, the son of the previous prison keeper, could make little sense of the man. The court-docket gave his name as Ignacio Damascus. Once out of the daylight in the gloom of the receiving cell, his skin took on a darker aspect, that of a lascar, come ashore no doubt from a ship from the Indies and taken to vagrancy. The man had no possessions to log. He seemed entirely indifferent to his incarceration. This was as much as Officer Ancell could conclude in the Reception Book.

The lascar was given a bowl of luke-warm soup and a piece of bread which he ate noisily in the receiving cell. Then he was led to the southern ward which housed the male prisoners. It being summer, the prison was relatively empty, so the new arrival was a cell to himself in the upper storey. Officer Ancell issued the man with prison greys patched with the number 111, and a blanket and a towel, and led him down to the bath house.
"Now bath!" he said, indicating the shallow stone trough of slimy water not unakin to the colour of the soup recently taken. There was no reaction to this instruction. Either the man did not understand this watering place was for bathing, or he was refusing his prison baptism. Officer Ancell was about to bark the instruction again. But there was no insolence, only a kind of dignity in the man's bearing that unsettled Mr Ancell, something to which it suddenly seemed impossible to issue an order. The officer looked once more at the man's garb, once more into his uninquisitive eyes, then marched him back into his cell.
"Put on these clothes!"
Again the order was ignored. Officer Ancell had no desire to wrestle with this foreign

vagrant over his paltry rags, from which a strange, sweet smell emanated, like cloying perfume.
"I'll be back in an hour and you'd better be wearing them", he barked, and locked the cell-door behind him. When he looked in through the judas-hole later that evening, and stole in to remove the fetid robes for the incinerator, the lascar was sound asleep, as if he had reached the destination for which he had set out, from God knows where, that morning.

It was left to the Chaplain, the Reverend Burnet, to establish some kind of rapport with the man in his initial interview the following morning. Upon unlocking the cell-door he found the prisoner on his knees at prayer, facing the window-grill of the cell. A lattice work of sunlight came through, dappling one wall, lending it a gentle, arboreal atmosphere. The honeyed lustre of the man's naked skin gleamed within it. A strange succession of pictures passed through the Chaplain's mind as he stood and witnessed the prisoner's devotions. A three-masted ship, a brilliant parakeet, a white feather falling through the air. The moment of meditative intensity was heightened by the discovery that the prayer the supine prisoner offered was a Christian one, and the language of it was Latin. The supplicant had concluded his prayer oblivious to its witness. The sign of the cross that sealed it proved conclusively that the bright-dark man before him was a Romanist. The Chaplain chose his greeting carefully.
"Salve!"
"Salve, Magister!" came the reply.
Now Mr Burnet was a highly educated man, with a thorough knowledge of Church Latin, but his colloquial command of the language was a different matter. As he wrestled with his opening vocatives, the lascar spoke in tones of quiet reassurance, more suited to the Chaplain's own role:
"Gentoa sum. I am Gentoa."
"You speak English?"
"Little. Sombetime. Welcome. Friend."
"You are a Catholic?"
"Yeb. Welcome."
This greeting countermanded the Chaplain's own welcome and made him feel rather indignant. He attempted to straighten out their confused roles in the cell by announcing his title.
"I am the Anglican Chaplain, Mr Burnet."
This seemed a matter of indifference or unfamiliarity to Gentoa.
"Where do you hail from? India? Gentoa Indian?"
"Portogallo."
"Portugese?"
"Gentoa from Goa."

Mr Burnet referred to his list copied from the Reception Book.

"You are Ignacio Damascus."

The lascar nodded, pointed at himself and spoke his name in fluent Portugese.

"Ignacio Caetano De Rozasia Damascus."

"Are you a sailor?"

"Sailor?"

"Ship?"

"Ship, yes. I am ship."

The ship and the Anglican priest eyed each other in the intensified quiet.

"In England you must not beg."

"Beg?"

"It is against the law."

Again this was met with indifference. The lascar pointed at the pencil poised over the Chaplain's notebook which he always carried into the cells.

"You give me, please."

Give me, give me, the daily cry of the prisoner. The Chaplain felt he was back on terra firma. To be able to turn down the request for the pencil re-established his authority quite simply and naturally.

"No. No writing. Today you must work. The magistrate says you must work. Law says you must work. Not beg. "

With the denial of the pencil there was the faintest flicker of malice, a first clue to the grasping, lazy criminal beneath such soft-spoken plausibility and religion. The lascar's next utterance was more of a cornered growl.

"I no work, damisize, I no work."

It was the same reply he had given Mr Ancell earlier that morning. Five minutes later Ignacio Caetano de Rozasia Damascus was under escort towards the refractory cell, flanked by Officers Ancell and Shepherd. In his report to the Governor, Mr Sanders, the Chaplain remarked on the man's obvious shrewdness and cunning which expressed themselves in a highly contaminating religious hypocrisy. He had interpreted the interjection as "damn His eyes" and thus as a blasphemy. But, charitably, he also did not admit to mention the stranger's gentility, which bespoke some learning, even if this learning had been thoroughly corrupted and misdirected. In his report, Officer Ancell recorded the disobeyance of orders and the repeated use of 'language'. The Governor had no hesitation in awarding the prisoner three days in the dark cell for refusing labour and for abusing both the Chaplain and the turnkey.

It was in the refractory cell that that Chaplain's second interview with the man who called himself Gentoa took place, on the fourth day of his imprisonment. Gentoa had not taken too well to solitary confinement. Turnkey Shepherd, who took charge of the refractory cells, had reported to the Governor that the lascar prisoner was subject to periodic ravings and outbursts of violent temper. The Chaplain had offered to intercede, as he felt a religious approach might be appropriate in softening the stranger's distress. The man's evident religion made the Reverend Burnet feel almost duty-bound to do so. But he was quite unprepared for the demonic vision that awaited him behind Gentoa's door, the direct antithesis of his first encounter.

The refractory cell was a stone room in the basement of the prison devoid of any light or furniture. As the door was unlocked, a stench assaulted his nostrils which the Chaplain was later to describe as the smell of human corruption itself. The very air around him seemed to swirl, to be filled with twisting skeins of impulses, hieroglyphs, symbols, with the two greenish eyes of Gentoa at their electric centre, blinking in the sudden intrusion of light. A warm draft suddenly seemed to buffet the Chaplain, almost extinguishing his candle. For a moment, Reverend Burnet fancied that he saw the substance of the prisoner's mind externalised in the cell, printing itself upon the atmosphere. He felt as if he had unearthed a necromancer, a demon in its lair. It was some moments before he could speak beneath the glare of those eyes.
"You must work today, Gentoa."
"Gentoa no work, damisize."
"That is a bad expression, Gentoa. You are a bad man. Work make you a better man. Treadwheel get rid of bad energy."
"Gentoa noble man. Dammim God know."
"That is blasphemy. Language injurious to God."
There was a silence between them and the swirling atmosphere around Gentoa was suddenly still. Another voice came out of him, not in the least irritable as before, but soft and coaxing.
"You give Gentoa."
Gentoa pointed to the pencil stub which the Chaplain carried with his notebook as he went from cell to cell.
"Gentoa write."
"Not allowed. No writing implements allowed. No messages!"
"Gentoa write. To God."
"You must pray to God, earnestly, to get you out of this cell." the Chaplain advised, "I am sure he will tell you to work, to work your way up from this pit of sin into which you have sunk."
"Gentoa no work! Dammim! No light!"
The prisoner came forward and blew out the candle defiantly. He was working himself into a rage again, and the Chaplain felt it was time to withdraw in case he proved violent. He called the turnkey. Evidently Gentoa had not had time to come to terms with his wicked thoughts. He must remain in the dark cell.

Stephen Plaice

"A rum one", the Chaplain said to Warder Shepherd once the door was closed, recovering his professional poise. Setting down his candleholder beneath the gas-lamp, he took out his leather-bound notebook. According to his notes, three of the other dark cells in the basement were occupied by the Brighton prostitutes who had caused an affray the previous Sunday in the Chapel. The incidence had been sparked off by the appearance of their bully, amongst the new intake of male prisoners. He checked his notebook for their initial interviews.

Mary Ann Loveridge…. led away by drink… no knowledge of our Saviour…. has been about the country - comes from Gloucester - kept a little huxter's shop, she says. Cries and talks a good deal plausibly - a very bad one I fear…..

Jane Parker … Knows her Redeemer's name but says "There's no use praying to God, I prayed as much as anybody and it never did me any good…. There is no use in believing anything about it." - Seems a very wicked woman…

Ann Mofs…strong Irish accent - (magistrate in Brighton gave her 10/- a week before as she was in search of her husband) - she then sought to get into prison to escape her bully…

Each time they came in such women would insist it was their first committal, though the Reverend had seen some of their faces as many as five times already during his Chaplaincy. They would pretend not to recognise him. These were Brighton, not local country girls. Seasoned prostitutes who had found their way to the town they know as London-by-the-Sea. For the most part they were hardened cases beyond redemption, and the Chaplain saw nothing in his notes that should detain him. But as he was about to leave the ward, he noticed the fifth door, the secure cell, was carded.

"Who's this?"
"New girl. Hysteric." Shepherd replied.
The Chaplain perused the card in the wooden plaque.
'CATHERINE WOOD. 1 MONTH IMPRIS.'
"Prostitute?"
Shepherd nodded.
"Hardly a beauty. Only came in this morning. Fought like a marten. Three days down here."
"A stranger?"
Shepherd shrugged.
"I'd best interview her."
The Chaplain relit his candle from the gas-lamp. The secure cell had an outer grill on

it as an extra security. He fumbled for the appropriate key on his ring. Warder Shepherd stepped forward obligingly to proffer his.
"Why the secure cell?"
"She is subject to fits, sir", Shepherd explained. "You must lock the outer gate behind you. I'll be just outside if you have any difficulty."
'Don't concern yourself", said the Chaplain, somewhat irritated by the man's presumption. "You may go about your business."

The epileptic was lying in a dishevelled state on the bare flagstones. She sprang to her feet with alacrity as soon as the light fell into the cell. But then shrank back at the sight of the Chaplain and curtsied to him vastly. She had the elfin features of the local girls, but her face was not known to him. It was bruised and there was a cast in her right eye. This could not have been more than her eighteenth summer. It appalled the Chaplain that one so young could have fallen.

"How is it, my child?"
"Cold, Reverend."
"But it's summer."
"Not in here."
"Have you ever been in a House of Correction before?"
"No."
"Do your parents know you are here?"
"No, I ain't seen 'em in a year."
"What is your parish?"
"The Ram Inn."

And here she laughed the laugh that incensed the Chaplain more than any other sound in the prison. It was the brazen laugh of the heathen delighted by its own salacity. It was not her own natural laugh. She had learnt from someone. It was the laugh of a London procuress. But more than one soul seemed to reside in this consumptive breast, because the laugh dissolved into a fit of coughing which ended in a look of contrition that would not have looked inappropriate on an icon of her namesaint unbroken on the wheel. There was an appeal in that look that said unequivocally to the Chaplain, "Rescue me from my contamination." He had seen that look countless times during his prison ministry, and he knew that if he could intervene swiftly, he might save them from the clutches of the Loveridges, the Parkers and the Mofs. The girl before him was much in need of catechization, and at this, the appropriate moment of their interview, he introduced the simple test of his own devising, to ascertain the degree of religious knowledge she already possessed. He asked five simple questions, and received five simple answers which he wrote down in his notebook.

"Who was our Saviour who died for our sins?"
"Cap'n Nelson."
"How did our Saviour die?"
"On a ship."
"Who made all things?"
"The East India Company."
"Who were the first man and the first woman?"
"Adam 'n' Eve."
"What does the Holy Spirit do for us?"
"Makes us tiddly."

The Devil in her waxed and waned in her answers. She was a haughty one, unashamed of her ignorance, almost willing him to chastise her for her disgraceful answers. Yet she continued to curtsy frequently and to call him 'your Reverence', even though it was plain she had none for his calling. Something in the girl's bruised face and flawed expression held him in the cell after the formalities of the interview were complete. With professional subtlety he modulated his tone from the admonitory to the pastoral, and slowly drew her story out.

"I comes from round 'ere.... but trawls about the country as many a girls do."
"What girls?"
"Why, those bad girls", she laughed, seeing his interest quicken, "that's how I get my bread. I goes with whoever comes."
"And then?"
"I do as I am told."
"What do they tell you to do?"
"Many a thing, many a bad thing."
"On the Sabbath?"
"On the stairway if they likes…"

She laughed the brazen laugh, then looked up to see if she had trespassed too far. She knew the responses to this litany and played the part well, as she had done with her customers, touching his arm at the appropriate moment.
"I just lift my skirts and…"
Her hands began to toy with the hem of her prison gown.
"…sets out my stall, your Reverence."
With a crooked smile, she slowly lifted the gown revealing a portion of white flesh underneath. Mr Burnet was transfixed, groping in his mind for words of censure. But

to his relief, the harlot's shame got the better of her and she dropped the gown again in another grotesque curtsy. No further word passed between them.

On leaving the cell the Chaplain was surprised to find a surfeit of Venus within himself. He paused a moment under the gas-lamp to master the unwelcome sensation. To distract himself from the residual image of whiteness beneath her gown, he took out his notebook and wrote:

'A very disturbed one... scant knowledge of her Redeemer... a temptress of the first water...'

He rearranged his cassock, cupped his hands over the offending stiffness, and moved awkwardly towards the inner gate where Turnkey Shepherd had stationed himself. The warder was eyeing him suspiciously.

"All in order Reverend?"
"All in order Mr Shepherd."

As Mr Burnet climbed the steps out of the dark cells, he could hear Gentoa wailing. He paused to listen. It was music of a kind, a sea-shanty he supposed, though he could make no sense out of the endlessly repeated refrain.

"Naheeni, nahaani, nahanna, naho..."

The lascar was singing from what seemed like the very bowels of the earth. Under Gentoa's spell for a moment, Mr Burnet saw again the brilliant parakeet of pleasure in his mind. Contamination was ever present in the prison. Not even he was immune. To counteract it, he gripped the cold iron rail of the prison landing tightly in his hand and tried to focus on the image of the Lord suffering on the cross. Then under his breath he repeated over and over the mantra with which he resisted temptation...

"Unclean spirit depart into swine! Unclean spirit depart into swine! Unclean spirit... depart... into swine!"

The antidote was, as ever, effective. And with his tumescence now subsiding, he repaired enthusiastically to luncheon with the Governor to discuss their forthcoming visit to Joshua Jebb's National Penitentiary which had recently been raised in the Capitol. Already the Separate System it introduced for prisoners had been widely praised. It would spell, at last, an end to contamination. And for this reason alone, both he and Mr Sanders were keen it should serve as their model for the New County Gaol.

Towards the end of the week an attempt was made to relocate Damascus in the main body of the prison. On a fine summer's morning he was fetched up blinking into the light and escorted by Turnkey Ancell to the Work Shed. But the sight of the tread-wheel and his fellow prisoners endlessly climbing it in their separate boxes drew a scream from Gentoa and a torrent of what was assumed to be Portugese. It was as if the mysterious sailor had been shown a glimpse of his ultimate fate in Hell. He refused to go within ten paces of the Wheel, let alone mount its steps. With terror in his eyes he turned to the gaoler and said,

"Dis be de factry of the deab."

Mr Ancell had no option but to return him struggling to the dark cell.

Catherine Wood fared a little better in her first week in the House of Correction. After her three days in the dark cell she was returned to the female ward and put in the charge of the Matron. The surgeon examined her and pronounced her unfit physically and mentally for any but the lightest labour. She was given linctus for her cough. The Matron put her to some sewing. She would eat very little, just bread and a few mouthfuls of gruel, which she pronounced very bad. Nevertheless, her quiet self seemed to be in command of her. When the Chaplain visited her he was able to draw more of her story from her.

"I am from the parish of Firle… all my family worked the estate when they could….my father had charge of the sheep sometimes…then my mother died….and I must go to work… I went to live in the Gage house there, in the scullery. The mistress was good to me. She taught me my letters. And I never took nothing that wasn't mine…

Here a fit of coughing came upon her that lasted a full minute. When she had finished, the poor contrite soul began again, in the meek tone of confession.

"But it was when the Railway men came to the village. One of them promised to marry me and take me to London if I let him. So I did. He used to come to the house. But after a two month the gang had gone and there was a new gang. I let them too - for five shilling. I needed the money to get rid of the baby…"

Here she managed to shed a few tears.

"…and then I went with them, trawling about the county…till I came to Brighton."

It was a familiar tale to the Chaplain who had long campaigned against the coming of the railway and, when it did come, for the strict policing of the navigators, many of whom had swollen his flock in recent years. But he could see there was good in the girl and still hope. She had some schooling and could read her letters. He left her a Bible and marked her a passage in Isaiah.

"All we like sheep have gone astray; we have turned everyone to his own way; and the Lord hath lain on him the iniquity of us all."

It was the same passage he chose as his text for the Morning Service that Sunday in the Chapel. As he surveyed his flock he was pleased to see his lost sheep in the centre of the female gallery. Her face had lost much of its bruising. She seemed almost demure amongst the raddled hags whose only interest in the service, he knew, was to catch sight of their bullies or common law husbands and to communicate with them. He felt an almost fatherly interest in the girl and feared for her in their company.

"…and he was numbered with the transgressors; and he bore the sin of many, and made intercession for the transgressors…"

He had reached that crucial moment in his exposition of Isaiah where he likened the condition of Christ to the condition of the transgressors before him when a fearful commotion began in their midst. All their heads turned from him towards the gallery. Catherine Wood was standing amidst the seated streetwalkers of Brighton, as if suddenly elevated to the level of their shoulders, with her skirts up around her waist, displaying her pudenda to the male prisoners below, shouting:

"Five shilling, five shilling, who wants it…"

It took two female warders and the Matron to remove the girl from the Chapel. The braying laughter above and below was uncontainable, and the Chaplain was forced to conclude his service in the most unfitting manner, with a hastily garbled prayer.

Every fourth day that month, Damascus was brought before the Governor and returned to the refractory cell for refusing to work the Wheel or in the Manufactory. There he languished by day on the bare floor, his bedding being removed to the bedding shed each morning by Turnkey Shepherd, and being returned to him at nightfall. But he did not sleep, he lay awake instead… listening to the incomprehensible whispering of the prostitutes through the privy-pipes, amidst the stench of the drains. Sometimes the warder heard him chanting monotonously, until the women called for him to be quiet. Towards the end of the month, when it was clear the lascar would see out the duration in the dark cell, the Governor instructed Turnkey Shepherd to permit the prisoner to retain his bedding during the day. But when checking the judas-hole the warder often found the man seated bolt upright, as

Stephen Plaice

if listening intently to something far away, 'to the sob of India' as Turnkey Shepherd expressed it one afternoon to the Reverend Burnet on his daily round.

"A very bad one, I fear I can do little for him" sighed the Chaplain in reply, opening the outer gate to the epileptic Catherine Wood and locking it behind him.

The Chaplain left Gentoa to his own devices. He visited him only once more, at the end of his month in solitary, shortly before he was due to be restored to the world. But this time their was no devilish apparatus in the air. All traces of the previous anger and malice had disappeared from Gentoa's voice. In the Reverend Burnet's view, the self-inflicted darkness had exerted a beneficial influence over the Romanist. The ship, as it were, had reached the harbour, albeit temporarily and in prison. During this last interview, Gentoa's thought took an almost philosophical turn, and his words, spoken in the seductive, mesmeric tone which complemented the best aspect of him, seemed to bind the Chaplain into their sense. These words were faithfully recorded in the leather-bound notebook.

"God made ebery thing. God made the good and God made the bad. God made the right hand and God made the left hand; left hand not so good as right hand; God made both. Eberything will come to good, bad will come to good, because God made it. He make what ebery man do. Christian three parts divinity, one part world; Gentoa three part world one part divinity."

And here Gentoa held out his long slender fingers, with their elongated curving nails, for the Chaplain's inspection.
"One man very bad."
He pointed to his little finger.
"Another a little good."
He pointed to his fourth finger.
"Another more good, another a little bad, another…"
He finished with the thumb.
"…no bad, all good, only passion, passion, that Gentoa. I no bad, no sin, only passion, then I'm sorry. I'm a noble man. Grace of God make me noble man. Dammim."
"No, Gentoa, not that word."
"Gentoa three parts Divinity Service and one part Unholy Service."
"Do you wish to get back to your own country?"
"Mercy from God - request for the world - I do a hope to get back soon."
The Chaplain was about to take his leave, but the lascar had the temerity to take his hand in a very firm grip. Mr Burnet felt the nails dig into his flesh and a pulsing force

surge through the human contact. For a second there was that same strange swirl of atmosphere in the light-dark cell, and Gentoa handed the Reverend Burnet the promised message from God.

It was pencilled on a tiny scrap of paper no bigger than a half crown. The cross was peculiar. A circle at the centre, four arms radiating from it. In each arm he had inscribed a letter of the alphabet. Reading from the top, the Chaplain was pleased to recognise the quaintly Romanist inscription. I.N.R.I. Here is the King of the Jews. In later years, the drawing, which on a whim the Chaplain preserved amongst his papers, was to remind him of the ground plan of the New Model Prison.

Having delivered his message from God, Ignacio de Rozasia Damascus departed the next morning on foot down the Brighton Road, dressed in unclaimed cast-offs Mr Ancell had rooted out from the stores. Both he and Turnkey Shepherd had developed a mild affection for their charge, patronising him with the name 'Sunny'. Before leaving Gentoa had elaborately thanked his keepers for his stay, still apparently oblivious to the nature of his incarceration. It is unclear how quickly he was able to find a ship to return to his own country. But there is no record of any subsequent arrest.

Catherine Wood outstayed the mysterious lascar by two days in the dark cells. After the outrageous fracas she had caused in the Chapel no further attempt was made to locate her in the main body of the prison. The Chaplain continued his ministry with her. Patient guidance and prayer seemed to have a calming effect on the girl, the longer she remained in the prison. The solitude wrought a change in her. At the end of her second week the Chaplain was surprised and delighted to discover that she had committed Isaiah 53 to memory. She recited it to him flawlessly and without embarrassment. She began to listen attentively when he read to her other significant passages from the Good Book, and sometimes to ask questions, even though still of a somewhat infantile nature. In the third week they focussed particularly on the Virgin Birth. The Chaplain answered as simply as he could.

"How come Mary was a virgin if she was wed to Joseph?"
"There had been no physical congress between them."
"How could she be with child?"
"That is the Mystery of Christ."
"Who was Jesus' real father then?"
"The Holy Ghost."
"How did the Holy Ghost come upon her?"
"He filled her from within."

Stephen Plaice

"What did it feel like?"
But the Chaplain did not answer this question, considering it unseemly and unworthy of her progress towards catechization.

In the final week of her sentence, on the same afternoon that Gentoa departed from the prison, Catherine announced to the Chaplain that she had seen the Holy Ghost.
"He was big and black and spoke like a piker."
The Chaplain smiled at her simplicity.
"No, that was Gentoa. You have seen Gentoa, the Romanist, in the neighbouring cell. A beggar off the ships."
"He came upon me."

The Chaplain had witnessed many such conversions amongst these Sussex people. It had been the last county to be Christianised, and he sometimes felt like a latter-day St. Augustine in his ministry to them. When their conversion came it was total and for the duration of their lives. The girl might be the victim of her own confusion in picturing the Holy Spirit as a black beggar. But the simple-minded needed pictures to understand things. What did that matter if her faith was strong, and she was set on the path towards goodness?

But Catherine Wood continued.

"And he told me to tell you something, your Reverend."
"A message?" He humoured her.
"A secret."
"A secret?"
"He told me to tell you that I have lied to you."
"Then let me hear your confession", the Reverend Burnet replied in a somewhat pompous Romanist manner.
"It wasn't a navvy-Jack who came to me. It was my father….after my mother died….my father came to me…"
"Yes?'
"He came upon me…I knew it were wrong…but he was my father…and the babe…after a four month I had to get rid of it…, it were a boy, it were my brother, Reverend"
A terrible silence had fallen in the cell and upon the Reverend Burnet. The Holy Spirit of Truth had indeed descended upon her. He could only watch the tear form and fall from the flawed eye and mutter:
"May God have mercy."
"But the Holy Ghost has made me clean again. He came to me here."

Her hand guided the Chaplain's own. He could feel the magnetism pulsing through her grip.
"He cleaned me here."

The following spring, Catherine Wood was received back into the prison, committed for aggravated vagrancy, sentenced to one month's hard labour. A sentence which was deemed inappropriate by Mr Turner the Surgeon, as she was in the eighth month of pregnancy. She was immediately accommodated in the Infirmary. Once installed there, she levelled an extraordinary accusation, namely that the child had been conceived during her previous term of imprisonment.
"I have brought the prison its child back."
When asked as to its paternity by the Matron, Catherine replied calmly:
"The Holy Spirit."

The Reverend Burnet discussed the prostitute's delusions with the Governor, over a glass of madeira. He recalled for Mr Sanders her epileptic confession from the previous year in which she claimed to have had congress with the Holy Spirit, in the shape of the lascar, Ignacio Damascus, known as Gentoa. At the time, the Chaplain had given no credence to her claim. But now, with the irrefutable fact of her pregnancy before them, he had to accept the fallen girl may have been telling the truth. Harlots were ever willing enough. Perhaps the lascar had indeed impregnated her.

Turnkey Shepherd was summoned to the Governor's office that same afternoon. At first he could shed no light on Catherine Wood's condition. He had not allowed the prisoners in the dark cells to fraternise or communicate. The only time they were left alone together was when he took their bedding to the bedding shed.
"Are their cells left unlocked?"
"No more than five minutes at most."
"Then that", concluded the Governor, "is doubtless when it happened."
Following his investigations, Mr Sanders issued a standing order:

"Forthwith each of the cells must be locked and unlocked individually when the bedding is removed and replaced in the refractory cells."

Turnkey Shepherd complied assiduously with the new regulation and continued with his normal duties for the rest of the month. But then, as April broke, so did Catherine Wood's water. On a sopping sheet in the Infirmary, the Matron delivered her of a boy, who, mysteriously, had none of the lascar in his face and was as fair as the harvest moon. Without further investigation, Turnkey Shepherd was given a month's pay and summarily discharged.

On Easter Sunday, Mr Burnet performed a Christian baptism for the bastard child in the Prison Chapel in the presence of the Governor. As the Chaplain took the baby in his arms and held it over the pudding bowl that served as a makeshift font, the hand that dipped for the holy water was visibly shaking. As he named the boy a white feather, no doubt from one of the feral doves that infested the rafters of the prison, fell mysteriously from the air. Catherine was proudly standing by, smiling her crooked smile. On Mr Burnet's advice, she had chosen the name John for the boy, after the Baptist. but former Turnkey Shepherd opined to his new-found friends in the Brighton beershops, the little beggar had been called Dick, after the Chaplain.

Cholera took Catherine Wood in the prison in the summer of 1843. In the orphanage her son was known to all as Prison John. It was only in his third year that it became clear he had a cleft palate. "As if," Chaplain Burnet ventured, "the Lord hath laid on him the iniquity of us all." Perhaps because of this impediment, when he was grown, the boy was deemed unfit for labour, he roamed about the country, but always in the lean winter months came back to his native county, and often to the prison, to the vagrants' ward. By many he was regarded as a simpleton, by a few, and magistrates among them, as an incorrigible rogue, even though the prison records show no worse crime than the theft of fruit against him in the sixty years of life he was granted. Entering his death in the register, at the turn of the century, the Rector of St. Anne's wrote against his name 'Born in the House of Correction.' He had perhaps the unique distinction of being born and dying in the prison, though by the time of his death, the gaol, now the New Model Prison, had been fifty years on its present site in the parish of St. Anne's. His fellow prisoners did not taunt him, despite his affliction. He was at home amongst them, and they could understand his speech, which the world without could not. In that dark place he seemed to have a kind of light in him that was not tallow. But neither was he the Baptist, nor the muted Christ. He too could steal his bread and fight when he had to, as every man must in prison. Yet no-one who knew him behind these walls, not even the succession of Chaplains he served in the Chapel, would have placed him as a bad character. He would have been counted, like so many of us here, on the middle finger of Gentoa's hand.

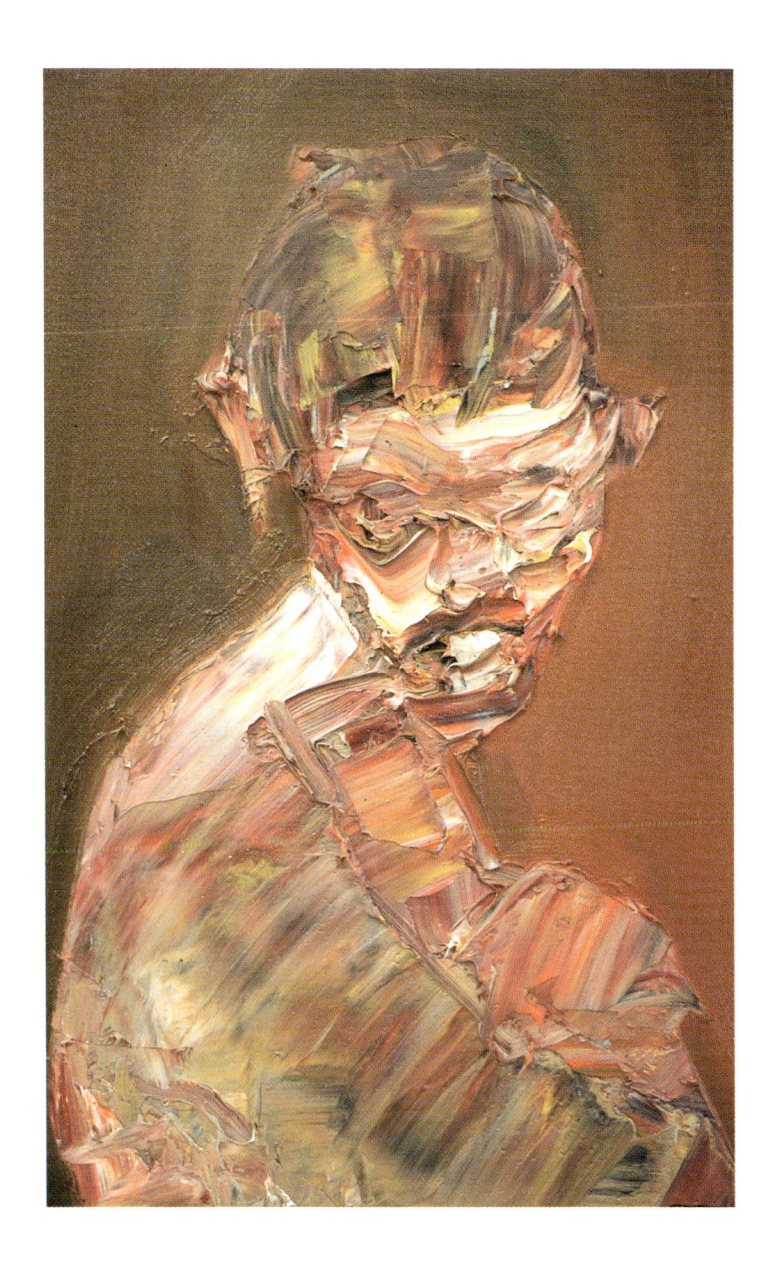

Plate 17   Di Kaufman. Sitter - Detail
              Oil on Canvas (18 x 14 in.)

Plate 18   Peter Messer. Boatbuilding and Astronomy
Tempera on Gesso Panel (24 x 16 in.)

Plate 19   Peter Messer. River of Secret Fish
Tempera on Gesso Panel (48 x 32 in.)
In the collection of David Pocock

Plate 20   Carolyn Trant. Autumn
Woodcut Print (20 x 16 in.) from the book *Gawain*
After the libretto by David Harsent

Plate 21   Carolyn Trant. I Am Not The Hero
Woodcut Print (20 x 16 in.) from the book *Gawain*
After the libretto by David Harsent

Plate 22 Tom Walker. All Who Come Here Come Here Alone
Soft Pastel on Black Paper (10 x 8 in.)
From *Purgations* - after the text by Mark C. Hewitt

Plate 23   Tom Walker. Ridiculous Ramshackle Edifice
Soft Pastel on Black Paper (30 x 20 in.)
From *Purgations*. (*In the collection of Mr & Mrs Lawes*)

Plate 24   Tom Walker. Submerged Cathedral
Soft Pastel on Black Paper (38 x 25 in.)
In the collection of Mr & Mrs Lawes

Untitled

I found my thrill in Nowheresville.

Culture is owned by the liars. Maybe that's not the way it used to be-- I'm not able to say-- and no one argues that it's the way that it should be. It's the way that it is now. Words are weapons in the hands of the social engineers, bureaucrats & propagandists. The Image is a shell & pea game designed to bilk the rubes. The common man is abandoned, left to his own devices, desperately scrabbling order & meaning together out of the flotsam & jetsam, and for all his efforts he is mocked by the media priests of the big lie. Scorn pours out and drowns the sticks and sand wall construction, overwhelming it with a flood of cynicism & a passion for the darkness.

Culture is a swampland of disinformation & half-truth. No critical faculty may be applied. We are dropped into the nightmare world of the internet: uncritical, undiscriminating and full of self-interest. The rantings of every village witch doctor are worthy. The scribbles of every Cambridge new-ager are valid. Culture is in the hands of the elite, the vested interest groups and the politicians. Because it can't be trusted it has no ordinary value. It is a form of terrorism.

[Folk Culture -- secret, nearly masonic-- is preserved in western culture but is disappearing in the "third world." The role of the media priests in this is understood by noting how they operate in a different field, such as popularizing the work of scientists & philosophers, and by considering, in quantum physics, what the effect of observation is on the observed phenomena.]

Geography is one heritage we can trust. The land speaks. Inorganic, it won't lie. Geography is also the things we add to the land. Our passing is etched across it. It gives answers. It asks questions. It forces puzzles. The truth is called a mirror. In it a man can see who & what he really is. Maybe the land is also like a mirror. The space we inhabit speaks to us not only of our hopes & fears but also those of our fathers & forefathers. What else is architecture but the means of embodying and preserving those hopes & fears? The space we inhabit cannot lie. We may only choose to not see.

Mark Twain wrote a book called *Life on The Mississippi*. It described the river & his days on it as a river pilot. It's a book about a river. A river means something. What it means endures & is passed from generation to generation. It collects to itself meaning as it passes thru time just as it adds to itself the flow of every tributary as it passes thru space. By the waters of Babylon I wept when I remembered you, Oh Zion. Take me to the river, wash me in the water. Down by the river I shot my baby. Springsteen's enduring work, *The River,* is fundamentally fuelled by that meaning.

What is a river? Is it a metaphor? How can that be? The device of the metaphor belongs to the world of the word; words are shadows. Is it a symbol? Not likely. You can't swim in a symbol or pull fish out of it. You can't sit by a symbol and feel the power of its peace and the inevitability of its flow or the electricity of its presence. A river finds its meaning in a language that has no words. (And so demands a medium beyond words.)

And you & I are connected to Mark Twain not because we share a bloodstock or genetic pool, or because of a political history, but because we share the river. The river does what it does and goes where it goes. Generation after generation it speaks. It's better than culture. There's no passing confusion about whether or not Mark Twain's family kept slaves. Or whether he was a white male with an oppressive cultural bias which needs redressing. They can screw with culture. They can't screw with a river.

I've seen abandoned gas stations, you see them everywhere, out in the middle of nowhere, and you ask yourself as you drive past, Why did anyone ever think to build that thing out here? Why? And you look around and see nothing.

It's 1957 and in New Mexico is a small town, or maybe it's Arizona. A man walks down a street without shadows. The dust is like perfume in the air. The man has a dream and a fear, one fear in his life. His dream is his wife. His wife is the one fear in his life. His one dream is his one fear.

That day the sun is like a broken lamp that buzzes too loud and shines too bright and there are no shadows in the man's life, everywhere hurts, and the place he's heading to doesn't seem to be so important to get to anymore. He stops at a bar where the air is dark and the nagging at the back of his neck is quiet for a time. He watches the top of his beer and listens. Eventually, he hears talk that's been going around town about how the government is planning a highway, a superhighway, and it's going down the middle of the valley.

All the world needs to go. All the world and his brother needs to be free. Gasoline is the currency of freedom.

If I can build myself a gas station out there where they're gonna put that superhighway, he says to himself, I will be a successful man. And a woman will love a successful man. I will build her a house on a hill. I will build her a swimming pool round back and she will dangle her feet in the water where she will see herself reflected and see how beautiful she is and know how much I love her. And the sun will flash in the water round her face and she will smile as my shadow falls across it.

This is the song the man sings at the stars one night as he sits on the porch of his gas station and watches the lights from the superhighway that the government built on the other side of the ridge.

People say, I wonder why
Why do stars twinkle in the sky?
Why do lovers ever have to say goodbye?
People say, I wonder why

People say, I wonder how
How do men & women ever get along?

People say, I wonder where
Where do the broken-hearted ever find to park their cars?
So many broken-hearted people
So many cars
All those headlights that search thru the night out on Mystery Road

Where can they go? Where can they wait out the night? So many cars. So few parking places. A man with foresight, he says to himself, would recognise this business opportunity. Such a man would grab it with both hands.

Heartbreak Garage. Build it and they will come. So many broken-hearted people.

David Thomas

Socks

She was tying her father's socks together
fashioning a long sky-blue chain with them
carefully testing each knot
singing to herself as she did so.
She was standing on a hilltop
holding the socks high above her head
watching them twist in the wind
like the colon of a disembowelled dragon.

She was in Margate picking dandelions.

She was walking down a broad suburban street at dusk
passing old plane trees
and the silvery arcs of lawn sprinklers.
A line of blue birds flew out across the sea
calling quietly to one another.
She was remembering a statue she'd seen
when she was a little girl
a unicorn in white marble
on a plinth by a bush near a small wooden bridge
that crossed a stream.
The moon was rising.
A man in a parked car was talking softly to himself.

She was rinsing her mother's dentures.

Hundreds of pieces of white paper
were falling through the air
as though autumn were a time of unread messages
and undiscovered meanings.
She was walking along a high stone wall.
The castle disappeared
the gardens the carpark and the bowling green
deckchairs stirring on a breezy patio.
There was only the sea
a long way below her
the cold gold moonlight of it
and a long twisting chain
of sky-blue fish.

The Old King

(To my father & my daughter)

We have come to pay our respects
to the old king
in his little white palace close to the sea
where roses bloom in yellow praise
walls remember candlelight and saints.

Today the old king
sits thin and frail on his throne.
His voice speaks from a heart so hushed
that words surrender to the silence they arise from.
You study his stiffening knuckles
his tentative step
with a child's dispassionate gaze.
You draw him a picture
of sunlight and rain
and the house where you live
as queen of the summer leaves
and the palace is filled with your rippling talk
the innocent light in your hair.
You reach for the world
the old king is slowly relinquishing
as his life draws into itself
like a symphony rinsed to its primal theme.

If he were here, down on the shoreline
he'd crouch in the breakwater lee
watching you wonder at details
wet stones brown as conkers
strands of net and kelp
damp limb of a dismantled dolly.
Then he'd lift his gaze
to contemplate the long horizon
where distant sea-birds ride the wind
and disappear.

Mutahar Williams

Mountain Train

Cornelius van der Stuffelgräffer
birds are singing in the lime trees
the shadows that gathered round your bed
have departed.
Truly there is nothing you need fear today Cornelius
a strudel in the kitchen and a pot of coffee
a thin cheroot for old time's sake
Rilke on the balcony
distills the juices of your ancient heart.

Death, they say, is just another season.
It's time to draw the curtains back
and let the roses reassure you.
Everybody knows what paradise was like
so put the photo album back where it belongs
take the mountain train
go catch some trout
and sniff the high blue air
for news of where it comes from.

I think I know your fears
at least my version of them.
Nothing can replace
the morning sunlight blazing in a bowl of apples.
But maybe there are other worlds to love
Cornelius
if we can truly say goodbye
to this one.

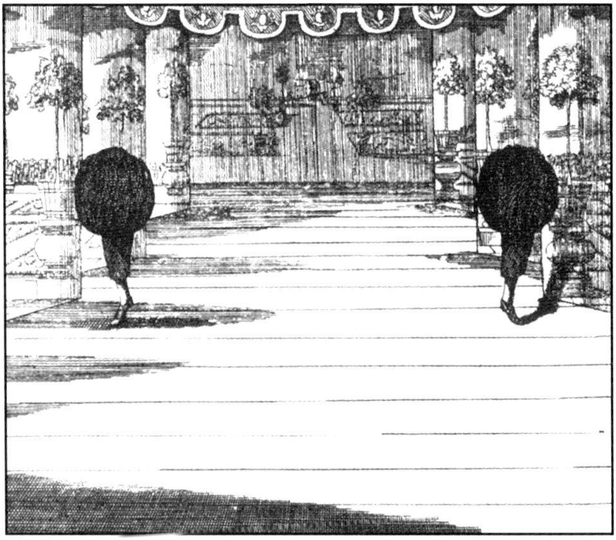

Biographical Details

Peter Abbs directs the MA in Language, the Arts and Education at the University of Sussex. He is also author of a number of books on education and culture and has published five volumes of poetry. He has given solo readings of his work during the Lewes Festivals 1995 and 1996 as well as a collaborative performance with composer Jonathan Harvey at the 1997 Festival and a collaborative event and exhibition with artist Lynne Gibson in 1995. The poems (with accompanying prints by Lynne Gibson) featured in this book are available as a limited signed edition of large hand printed booklets from Snake River Press, 1 Wilbury Gardens, Hove, East Sussex BN3 1AU. Peter Abbs lives in Lewes. The poems (without the prints) can also be found in *Personae and other selected poems* (Skoob Books, 1995).

John Agard was born in Guyana and came to Britain in 1977. Acknowledged as a warm and direct poet he won the Casa de las Americas prize in 1982 and a Paul Hamlyn award in 1997. As a touring speaker with the Commonwealth Institute he visited nearly 2000 schools promoting Carribean culture and poetry, and has since performed on television and around the world. In 1993 he became the first Writer-in-Residence at London's South Bank Centre and in 1998 the first Poet-in-Residence on the BBC Network. He is also a popular children's writer and playwright. A resident of Lewes he has performed at the 1995 and 1996 Lewes Festivals. The poems in this book come from his most recent collection *From the Devil's Pulpit* (Bloodaxe, 1997) and his South Bank Collection *A Stone's Throw from Embankment*.

Julian Bell has worked as a self-employed painter for the last twenty years and has been based in Lewes since the early eighties. His visual work is represented by the Francis Kyle Gallery, London W1. He also reviews painting for the TLS and Modern Painters and is the author of *Bonnard* (Phaidon, 1994). His poems have appeared in various magazines and a first volume *Three Odes, A Tale & A Bad Poem* was published by Lewes based Dale House Press in 1997. For Lewes Live Literature he has given readings of his work at the Lewes Festival 1997 and at the launch of a joint *Marriages of Word & Image* exhibition with Carolyn Trant in 1996.

Peter Blegvad is a writer, illustrator, cartoonist and singer/songwriter. Born in New York City in 1951 he has spent much of his life in the UK. Since 1991 he has been contributing the cartoon *Leviathan* to the Independent on Sunday. As a singer/songwriter he has produced five solo albums, most recently *Just Woke Up* (Recommended, 1996), and is well-known by many for his pioneering work amongst the rock and roll avant garde of the 1970's and 80's with bands Slapp Happy, Faust, Henry Cow and The Golden Palominos. His most recent book of writings and drawings, *Headcheese* was published by Atlas Press (London, 1994). In 1996 he contributed to the Lewes Live Literature *Marriages of Word & Image* series with his lecture and exhibition *Imagined, Observed, Remembered*.

Gordon Bowker is the author of the definitive biography of Malcolm Lowry: *Pursued by Furies* (Harper Collins, 1993) plus a number of other books and radio broadcasts treating the same subject. He gave a talk in Lewes in November 1997 to launch an exhibition by artist Peter Messer commemorating the 40th anniversary of the author's death in Ripe and the fiftieth anniversary of the publication of his masterpiece, *Under the Volcano*. Gordon Bowker has also written a biography of Lawrence Durrell, *Through the Dark Labyrinth* (Sinclair Stevenson, 1997/Pimlico Press, 1998), and is currently working on a novel and on a book about writers in the 1930s. As a journalist he has contributed to the Observer, Sunday Times, Listener, TLS, Illustrated London News and Plays & Players, as well as writing and presenting arts and other radio documentaries for the BBC.

Martin Cooper was born in 1956 and grew up mainly in the South of England including seven years in Sussex where he went to school in Lewes. Since then he has lived in the north of England, first in Manchester currently in Newcastle where he teaches English at a comprehensive school. In his poetry he seeks to evoke the inspiration that is to be found in the mountains and in climbing as well as celebrating some of the wild places still to be found in Britain. His first collection, *Fire on the Mountain,* was published by Cliffe Bookshop, Lewes, in 1997.

Peter Copley, a composer, was born in Hove in 1962. After studying at the Royal Academy of Music and privately with the late Hans Keller, a Polish Government scholarship took him to the Akademia Muzyczna in Krakow. This proved to be the beginning of an enduring connection with Eastern Europe, from where he has received many of his most significant commissions and first performances. Recent works include a Wind Quintet, a Concerto for Trumpet, Strings and Percussion and 'No Man's Land' for two double basses. A Violin Concerto was first performed in the 1997 Lewes and Brighton Festivals and is planned to be released as a CD by Claudio Records. Recent projects include a string sextet for the performance project

Purgations with Mark Hewitt (text) and Tom Walker (images), and a Lewes Live Literature commission *Cascando*, reworking a 1960's Beckett radio play for two voices and music.

Lol Coxhill has been playing saxophone professionally since 1952. He is most well-known for his freeform improvisational solo work but has composed extensively for theatre and film projects, including Derek Jarman's *Caravaggio* and a spell as Music Director for Welfare State Theatre Company. In 1985 he was the subject of an Arts Council documentary film *Frogdance*. Various recordings of his music have been released in Britain, Europe, Japan and the USA and he has guested on and supported many famous acts, including (during the sixties) Martha & the Vandellas, Wilson Pickett, Screaming Jay Hawkins and B.B. King and later The Damned, Frank Chickens, Spontaneous Music Ensemble, Otway & Barrett and others. He first performed in Lewes during the Brighton Festival 1997 in a show which included a rare performance of his playlet *Murder in the Air*.

Greg Daville is a visual artist and writer. He studied at the Royal College of Art and has exhibited his work in galleries throughout the country, including Angela Flowers, the ICA, the RA and Riverside Studios. His work for a number of years has explored the exhibition of text in galleries, with *Pictures to Imagine*, *Beautiful Crazy Happiness Inc.* and other shows. Two collections of writing, *90 Neatly Written Lies* and *Double Glazing the Large Glass* are now part of the Victoria & Albert Museum's library collection and *Pictures to Imagine* is in the Printed Matter Archive, New York. He also has work in Ian Breakwell and Paul Hammond's Penguin anthology of new writing *Brought to Book*. He performed his work at the Lewes Festival 1995 and his performance work *Building Platforms from which to Fall* formed the basis of a Lewes Live Literature *Marriages of Word & Image* exhibition in 1996. He is currently working on a first novel *Harbinger's Net*, an early draft of which is sampled in this book. *The Entertainers* was designed by Greg Daville.

John Dowie is a Brighton based writer, performer and director. Previously recognised more for his work as a comic writer and comedian he gave his first performance as a poet at the Lewes Festival 1996. He has written widely for television and radio and collaborated in the past with many of the big names in contemporary light entertainment including Rory Bremner, Neil Innes and Victor Spinetti. He has also directed two stage adaptions of poems by Heathcote Williams: *Whale Nation* and *Falling for a Dolphin* plus children's shows *Dogman* and *Poems To Read To Your Parents*. Solo shows include *Take Them To The Garden*, (based on the life and works of Philip K. Dick) and *Why I Stopped Being a Stand-up Comedian*. His recent play *Jesus - My Boy* is currently being produced for the West End and Broadway with Tom Conti as Joseph.

Andy Gammon is a graphic designer, illustrator and artist who has been living and working in Lewes since 1975. He was born in Canterbury in 1947 and attended the Canterbury College of Art from 1965-1969. After working in London in the early 70s, producing posters and programmes for the fledgling Other Cinema and then in a design studio, he left for the south coast where he worked in various studios and design workshops before setting up his own practice in 1981. His enduring interest in history and has lead him into historic interpretation displays in museums and archaeological sites around the country. From an early age he has maintained an active interest in figure drawing, mono printing, etching and wood engraving culminating in an exhibition at the Lewes Artwave Festival, 1997.

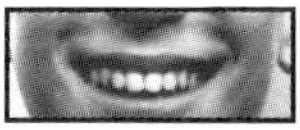

Doj Graham. Born 1953.

Lynne Gibson is a painter and printmaker currently living in Gloucestershire. Her work, including the prints made in collaboration with poet Peter Abbs as featured in this book, were the subject of the first Lewes Live Literature *Marriages of Word & Image* exhibition in 1995. She has shown in Sussex and across the UK, including at the Fiveways Open Houses in the Brighton festival and at the RWA in Bristol. Galleries include Christie's Contemporary Art, The Oxford Gallery, Dexterity Gallery in Cumbria and Rye Art Gallery. Born in Brighton in 1957 she read for an MA at the University of Sussex and held a lectureship in Critical Studies. She maintains strong links with the area including teaching Continuing Education vacation courses in Painting at the Gardner Arts Centre.

Tony Haase wrote and first performed his comic monologue *The Black Room* (directed by John Dowie) at the Brighton Festival 1993 where it won Best Comedy Award. Originally trained as a fine artist, Tony was a long-term member of the Brighton-based Cliffhanger Theatre Company, co-writing and performing many shows, including *They Came From Somewhere Else* (which became a six-part series for Channel 4), *Gymslip Vicar* (nominated for Best Comedy Olivier S.W.E.T. Awards) and the sitcom *Mornin' Sarge* for BBC2. He is a lifelong partner in the 'Les & Robert' duo with Robin Driscoll. His TV work includes appearances on *Colin's Sandwich*, *The Day Today*, *Knowing Me Knowing You*, *Saturday Night Armistice* and Vince in the 'Do-It-All' adverts.

David Harsent has published six collections of poems. His *Selected Poems* appeared in 1989, and his most recent collection, *News From the Front* was published in 1993. His libretto for Harrison Birtwistle's opera *Gawain*, the world premiere of which was held at the Royal Opera House, Covent Garden, in 1991, inspired the set of prints that comprise the artist's book *Gawain* by Lewes-based printmaker Carolyn Trant. David Harsent's English versions of poems written under siege by the Bosnian poet Goran Simic, *Sprinting from the Graveyard*, was published by OUP in March 1997 and was the basis of his reading (with actress Julia Watson) at the 1997 Lewes Festival. His new collection, *A Bird's Idea of Flight*, was published by Faber & Faber in March 1998.

Jonathan Harvey is a composer with a worldwide reputation for his imaginative and innovative electronic music which has attracted commissions from a host of international organisations and is regularly performed at the major contemporary music festivals by the Ensemble Intercontemporain and other major ensembles. Born in Warwickshire in 1939, he was for 18 years Professor of Music at the University of Sussex where he is now Honorary Professor of Music. He is also the permanent part-time Professor of Composition at the University of Stanford in the USA. Much of his output has been recorded and he has a number of CDs devoted exclusively to his music. Recent works include a BBC-commissioned *Percussion Concerto* for Evelyn Glennie premiered at the 1997 BBC Proms and *Ashes Dance Black* for choir and electronics, first heard at Strasbourg Musica 97. During the 1997 Lewes Festival Jonathan Harvey gave a Lewes Live Literature performance in collaboration with poet Peter Abbs.

Drew Hewitt, born 1960, is an artist and writer. His paintings, drawings and prints have been shown throughout the country in group and solo exhibitions and he has work in several major collections. He studied fine art at Leicester Polytechnic and film production with the National Film and Television School. As a writer Drew has concentrated on projects for film, television and the stage. Film scripts include *The Monkey Painter* and *Mutt*, and stage plays include *White Like Snow* and *Come Again*. His lecture *Berts, Toms, Jacks & a Sig* was first given as part of the Lewes Live Literature *Marriages of Word & Image* series in 1996. A lecturer in Art, Art History and Media Studies, he currently lectures at Alton College in Hampshire.

Mark Hewitt is a poet and the founder and artistic director of Lewes Live Literature. His current poetic projects include a cross-art performance piece, *Purgations*, combining spoken text with projected images by visual artist Tom Walker and music (for string sextet) by Peter Copley; due also to be released in book form. He is also working on a collection of landscape and figure texts that combine descriptive elements with meditations on mortality and *The Grotesque Projec*t, a public art initiative combining a short 5 line verse with a sequence of corresponding architectural grotesques. He works as a project co-ordinator and literature development worker for the Sussex Literature Development Network and other organisations and is a literature adviser for South East Arts Board.

Pierre Hollins has performed on the alternative cabaret circuit for many years. He has written for TV and radio and his cartoons have been published in England and America. He wrote sand performed his show *How To Rule The Planet* for the Lewes Festival 1996.

Nicki Jackowska is the author of five collections of poetry and four novels. The poems in this book are taken from her new collection, *Spikenard* and will also be included in *Lighting a Slow Fuse - New and Selected Poems* to be published by Enitharmon in September 1998. She has worked regularly with artists in other media, both as tutor and performer, including a collaboration with traditional Irish band 'Moving Clouds'. Her 25 years' experience writing, performing, broadcasting and tutoring creative writing are encapsulated in her recently published *Write for Life* (Element, 1997), a creative writing manual and radical exploration of language, identity and relationship.

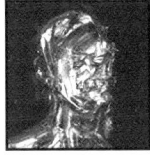

Di Kaufman, born 1944, began studying art in her forties. By the time of her graduation from the Kent Institute of Art and Design she knew that she wanted to work in that tradition of painters that culminated in the work of Bacon and Auerbach: the depiction of the human figure. Her first solo exhibition, (the sixth in the Lewes Live Literature *Marriages of Word & Image* series), was entitled *Envelope of Flesh* and was launched with a series of readings evoking a sense of flesh and physicality. Di lives in Kent.

The Entertainers

Mimi Khalvati was born in Tehran in 1944 and educated in England where she attended Drama Centre London and the School of African and Oriental Studies, University of London. She has worked in the theatre, acting and directing and has co-translated plays from English into Farsi. She is now a visiting creative writing tutor at Goldsmith's College and a regular tutor on the Arvon Foundation writing courses. She has published three full collections of poetry, most recently *Entries on Light* (Carcanet, 1997). She has given readings all over Britain and taken part in reading tours of the Czech Republic and Spain. Her poems have been broadcast on BBC Radio 3 and 4 and Radio Scotland. Mimi read at the Lewes Festival 1997. She lives in London and is Coordinator of The Poetry School.

John May has worked as a freelance writer in all areas of publishing for the last 20 years. His work has appeared in the New York Times and most of the major broadsheet papers and supplements in Britain. He has authored, co-authored, edited or produced thirteen books. His current points of focus oscillate between the 21st Century and the 19th. He is writing for the Daily Telegraph's weekly technology supplement *Connected*, and building web sites for his company Cequel Plus. On the other hand he is Project Director of the Rodin 2000 initiative which has succeeded in getting the Tate Gallery's agreement to lend Rodin's *The Kiss* to the town of Lewes, (its original home), for a millennium exhibition.

Grace Nichols was born and educated in Georgetown, Guyana, but has lived in Britain since 1977. In 1983 she won the Commonwealth Poetry Prize with her first book of poems, *i is a long-memoried woman*. Since then she has published three more collections of poetry, most recently *Sunris* (Virago, 1996) which won the Guyana Prize for Poetry, and a novel, *Whole of a Morning Sky* (Virago, 1986). Her most recent book for children was *Asana and the Animals* (Walker, 1997). Her other children's books include two collections of short stories, two books of poems and a number of anthologies. She has given many readings of her poetry in Britain and around the world and been the subject of a TV profile. She lives in Lewes with the poet John Agard with whom she performed at the Lewes Festival 1995.

Stephen Plaice is a regular scriptwriter for Thames' *The Bill*, many of his stories for which are influenced by his experiences working as Writer-in-Residence at Lewes Prison. He also works for *Dreamteam*, Sky TV's new football drama. His plays include *Home Truths* and *Trunks*, about the infamous Brighton Trunk Murders. his play *The Last Post* was made into a BAFTA nominated short film. He is also the librettist for *Misper*, Glyndebourne's teenage opera, premiered in 1997 and revived in 1998.

Paul Taylor is a fireman and photographer.

David Thomas is known most widely for his work with legendary rock band Père Ubu. Born in Miami, Florida in 1953, the son of an American Literature Professor and botanical illustrator, Thomas first founded Père Ubu in 1975, subsequently recording five studio albums and numerous singles. In 1981 he began a solo career working with various combinations of instruments and musicians allowing space for increased improvisational and solo spoken word elements. He recorded five solo albums between 1981 and 1986 before reforming Père Ubu for further touring and recording projects. David Thomas first performed in Lewes in 1996 with his improvisational music ensemble *Two Pale Boys*, returning for a solo performance during the Lewes Festival 1997. He currently lives in Sussex.

Carolyn Trant is a painter and printmaker whose work is about landscapes and the history, myths and stories associated with them. She has worked with archaeologists looking at new ways of considering the landscape, and recently has started making Artist's Books (under the imprint Parvenu Press) as a way of presenting sequences of images that are designed to be kept together. In 1995 she produced a book of etchings with Peter Chasseaud entitled *Caburn*. Her second book, *Gawain*, was produced as a response to seeing the opera by Harrison Birtwistle, using words from the libretto by the poet David Harsent. Carolyn has had many exhibitions locally and in London of her tempera paintings, drawings and prints. She teaches printmaking at the Paddock Studios in Lewes.

Tom Walker, born 1949, is a visual artist working in most 2D media, with a particular interest in pastel and acrylic. Much of his work over the last 20 years has been created in response to music, particularly the organ works of French composer Charles Tournemire (1870-1939), whose monumental cycle of organ masses (*L'Orgue Mystique*) he responded to in kind with a cycle of triptychs in pastel on black paper, the framing for the project being funded by the composer's widow. Several of these images are reproduced on CD's of Tournemire's music, with others in preparation. In addition to regularly touring exhibition/recitals with organists to churches and cathedrals in Britain and Europe, he has also collaborated with

The Entertainers

musicians on simultaneous classical and jazz improvisations. Tom's work has been exhibited widely and is in collections in France, Germany Italy, Holland, Hungary, the USA and Britain. Current projects include a cross-art collaboration with Mark Hewitt (text) and Peter Copley (music) as part of the performance project *Purgations*, for which he also designed the set, and a 120 foot mural on music by Debussy.

Mutahar Williams has written and produced radio and TV programmes for children and adults in both Britain and California and produced films and videos of his nature poetry combining visuals, words, natural sound and music. He has performed his poetry, often in a multi-media context, to audiences in arts centres, universities, colleges, theatres, pubs and cafés all over the world. His most recent book, *Witness*, (with etchings by Sofiah Garrard) was published by Windwords Press in 1993. More recently he has released a CD (*Sock*s) of his poetry with musical accompaniment. He lives in Lewes.

Lewes Live Literature welcomes feedback and response to this book. Should you wish to communicate with LLL Publications or any of the contributing writers or artists please send your letters c/o Lewes Live Literature, All Saints Centre, Friars Walk, Lewes, East Sussex BN7 2LE.

Where no biographical information is supplied the artist specifically does not wish to provide any.